PRAISE FOR *Dr,*

MW00572401

"Josh Stumpenhorst is back with a fresh take on common classroom challenges. If you believe your students are lazy, unmotivated, or apathetic, maybe you need to take a hard look at your classroom—and yourself. Stumpenhorst's rollicking illustrated guide, *Drawn to Teach*, will guide you toward more effective classroom management, lesson planning, and student relations with tips that will exhilarate you and your students."

—Daniel H. Pink, author of *Drive* and *When*

"Josh Stumpenhorst uses an unconventional approach of illustration and words to provide adaptable solutions for pressing instructional issues. This book responds to the needs of students while positioning the educator as a learning partner. Few books have staying power, but *Drawn to Teach* will be as relevant years from now as it is today. Count on me to encourage educators from across the country to make this book a critical resource."

—Harriet Sanford, president and CEO, The NEA Foundation

"Josh Stumpenhorst has created a visual masterpiece to guide educators through the process of change. Using the power of imagery, he tackles concepts that are at the heart of a school's learning culture while providing practical strategies for growth and improvement. His creative style not only tackles pressing problems that all educators experience, but also fleshes out solutions that can be readily implemented. If you like comics and learning, then this book is for you."

—Eric Sheninger, best-selling author and senior fellow with the International Center for Leadership in Education (ICLE)

"Josh Stumpenhorst's *Drawn to Teach: An Illustrated Guide to Transforming Your Teaching* is a fresh, fun challenge to teachers who want to up their game and invigorate their practice. Filled with clever, relatable examples, *Drawn to Teach* reminds us to keep kids at the center of our decision-making and to let our students' talents and passion lead the way. Like the proverbial frog in hot water, sometimes teachers don't realize their pedagogy and practices need tweaking until it's too late. Let *Drawn to Teach* and Stumpenhorst's sage advice help you turn down the heat and turn you back on to why you became a teacher in the first place."

—**Rebecca Mieliwocki**, 2012 California and
National Teacher of the Year

Drawn to Teach
©2019 by Josh Stumpenhorst

All rights reserved. No part of this publication may be reproduced in any form or by any electronic or mechanical means, including information storage and retrieval systems, without permission in writing by the publisher, except by a reviewer who may quote brief passages in a review. For information regarding permission, contact the publisher at books@impressbooks.org.

This book is available at special discounts when purchased in quantity for use as premiums, promotions, fundraisers, or for educational use. For inquiries and details, contact the publisher at books@impressbooks.org.

The author has tried to recreate certain events, locales, and conversations from his memory. Names, physical characteristics, and identifying details have been altered to protect the privacy of individuals. Some sections of this book include names, characters, places, and events that are part of the author's imagination. In these instances, any resemblance to actual persons or events is purely coincidental.

Published by IMPress, a division of Dave Burgess Consulting, Inc.

ImpressBooks.org

daveburgessconsulting.com

Editing and Interior Design by My Writers' Connection

Cover Design by Trevor Guthke

Library of Congress Control Number: 2019933756

Paperback ISBN: 978-1-948334-08-2

eBook ISBN: 978-1-948334-09-9

First Printing: March 2019

DEDICATION

I dedicate this book to any teacher who is working and doing their best by kids. Especially those who can see past the gimmicks, fads, trends, and knows the tremendous gift and responsibility it is to work with young people.
—Josh

I dedicate this book to my wife, Amy, who is always by my side. Whenever I am struggling in this life, she is by my side with words of support. Whenever I am driving, she is by my side, yelling at the kids. Whenever I am drawing, she is by my side, killing virtual zombies on her smartphone.
Thanks for your patience with me, baby!
—Trevor

CONTENTS

FOREWORD
BY QUINN ROLLINS

When I heard Josh Stumpenhorst was writing another book for teachers, I was excited. Then I heard that his new book had graphic novel elements, and I knew I had to have it. Josh is one of the first educators I followed on Twitter, and I felt like I was always getting ideas from his feed that I could implement in my own middle-school classroom. Over the years, he's been one of the teachers who's been a source of inspiration, showing the power of a PLN even if you're several states away.

I'm fifteen years into my teaching career, and this was the perfect book for me to read at this particular time. There are so many books out there for teachers who are just getting started—*Drawn to Teach* is good for early teachers but also perfect for a veteran teacher who needs a refresh. It's a reminder of the evergreen fundamentals of education, leavened with concrete strategies that can help you today in the classroom.

I use graphic novels and comics with my students, and I have seen their power firsthand. As with many other educational innovations, if it's good for the kids, it's probably good for their teachers. The illustrations help make *Drawn to Teach* a funny and unique take on professional learning.

The graphic-novel-style "case studies" are a great way to relate to the characters and scenarios—we see these teachers in every school, and sometimes those teachers are us. More than once while reading the book, I thought, "Oh man, I know that guy, he needs to shape up," and then, a few pages later, was blushing because I *was that guy.* This illustrated insight into how the teachers are handling challenges is lightened with some humor, but the point is clear—we all have work to do. The knack Josh has is helping us see that we're up to the challenge. We can do it.

Another benefit of the graphic novel style is being able to see the "thought bubbles" of the teachers and the students. Those bubbles let us see that often, while a teacher is in front of the room "teaching," students are focused elsewhere. We can see the thoughts of the teachers in the faculty room simmering over another teacher's test scores, feeling underappreciated or even threatened. We don't get to see those thought bubbles in our real world; seeing them here reminds us that there are other perspectives besides our own.

Drawn to Teach has a focus on the social and emotional needs of our students—that our content is important, but knowing the students and knowing how to respond to their needs takes precedence over our mandated curriculum. Knowing them as kids comes before teaching them as students. Every kid has a story. Knowing their stories will make a better classroom.

More than anything, this book gives us permission to take risks, to make changes, to teach with intention. If you've made some missteps in the classroom (And who among us hasn't?), you can get back on track. It's not too late to innovate. It's not too late to find motivation. It's not too late to grow. As you sit down with *Drawn to Teach*, get ready to smile and have fun as you learn.

QUINN ROLLINS IS A HISTORY TEACHER IN SALT LAKE CITY, UTAH, AND AUTHOR OF *PLAY LIKE A PIRATE: ENGAGE STUDENTS WITH TOYS, GAMES, AND COMICS.*

INTRODUCTION

The premise of this book was born out of my love for graphic novels and the fact that, as a medium, it is woefully underutilized in professional texts. When I first read *The Adventure of Johnny Bunco* by Daniel Pink, I wondered how I could create a similar book for educators. Thus was the start of *Drawn to Teach*. Thankfully, a good friend of mine, Trevor, had the artistic and creative chops to make my vision come to fruition. The goal of this book is not to be gimmicky or pretend to speak from a place of superiority in teaching. It is simply a collection of stories, ideas, and research that gets to our core values of teaching.

The format of the book is unique and, admittedly, was a lot of fun to create. Each chapter starts with a graphic novel narrative of a teacher, or handful of teachers, in their classrooms or schools. The stories each address a core value we embrace within education: relationships, technology, professional growth, teaching what matters, motivation, and innovation. After each story, there is a short section titled "Frame Your Reading," which allows the reader to stop and reflect on the narrative graphics before getting into the text content. The text content is then broken down into a problem-and-solution format. Through identifying the problems our teacher characters encounter, we construct common sense and research-based solutions for teachers. After the "meat" of each chapter, we pose more questions for deeper reflection and discussion of the chapter's content. In addition, we have created a list of things you can do tomorrow when you walk into your school or classroom. Finally, we have an administration section. This will be where we provide tips for administrators, noting how you can help your staff move forward in these core value areas.

Between the chapters, you'll find short interludes that we've titled "It Will Happen." These frames and stories feature events and occurrences that happen in a classroom, along with some sound advice on how to handle each of them effectively.

We do not pretend to have all of the answers, nor do we think education is about seeking out right or wrong answers. Rather, our goal in this book is to create conversations around real problems teachers face and give practical and impactful solutions. Any educator who reads this book should be able to take something into their school or classroom tomorrow.

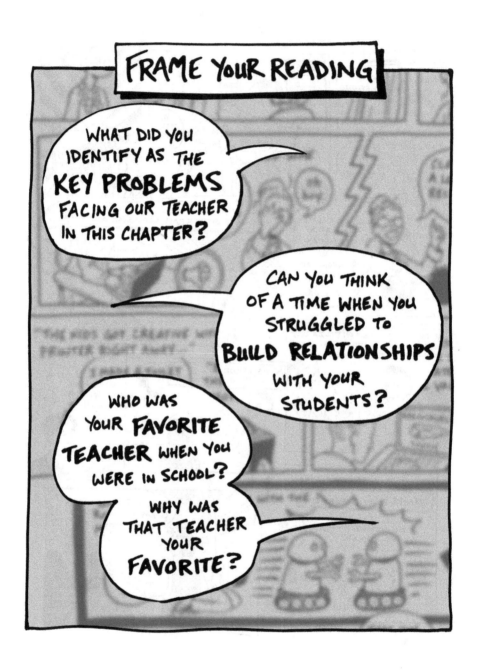

Teachers make many mistakes when it comes to working with students, one of which involves getting into a power struggle with them. Too often, this struggle stems from a teacher's failure to form positive relationships with students built on mutual understanding and respect.

FRAMING THE PROBLEM

● PROBLEM ONE: CLASS RULES

Creating classroom rules is something every teacher has likely experienced as a student themselves or overseen in their own classroom. Our teacher, Mr. Pape, opens the school year by focusing on his classroom rules, which he thinks will ultimately help him have a great year. This is a common theme with teachers. Classroom walls around the globe are adorned with classroom rules. Many of these rule lists are created by the teacher with little or no input from the students they are meant to "control." To be clear, a set of rules or expectations is critical to maintaining a safe learning environment within a school or classroom. However, the manner in which they are created, along with how they are reinforced, is critical to the success of the rules. Rules and classroom expectations can lay the groundwork for a positive classroom culture with the student/teacher relationship at the heart.

● PROBLEM TWO:
DISINTERESTED STUDENTS

No matter what age group or subject matter you teach, you will inevitably have students who are just not interested in what you are teaching. In the middle of page three of our comic, Mr. Pape yells at two students in the back of the room for talking. He doesn't even care to find out what they are talking about, but rather assigns them a punishment and sends them on their way. The aftermath is immediate, as the students complain in the hallway about the teacher, as well as the resulting discipline both at school and impending at home.

While students should certainly be respectful during class, this paints a clear picture of what can happen when students are bored or not interested in the content being taught. The root cause of disinterested students is typically one of two things. First, the content is being presented in a manner which does not connect with the student on a personal level. Some kids can overcome this, but many just tune out. Another reason for disinterested students is the presented content being either too difficult or too easy. If the teacher is asking students to do something incompatible or inconsistent with their skill sets, they are more likely to tune out. Getting to know your students, and having positive relationships with them, can alleviate the issue of disinterested students. This will help teachers get to know their students' interests and abilities to direct or adjust classroom instruction accordingly.

● PROBLEM THREE: SHAMING KIDS

Shaming students is something that should never be utilized by a teacher, and yet we see it happen all the time. Mr. Pape shows us this on page four when some of his students do not turn in their work. The value of homework aside, kicking the students out creates a handful of problems that make it more difficult for the teacher to connect with students.

First, many students would find being put in a situation like this embarrassing. They would not want to be the center of attention, particularly not for a negative reason (such as being dismissed from class). This will further distance the student from the teacher. In addition, this can breed mistrust in the student, which will be hard for the teacher to overcome.

Conversely, it is possible some students relish the attention, even if it is negative. This is also problematic for the teacher, as it reinforces negative behaviors. Students who seek negative attention are emboldened by the teacher's actions and will continue to seek it out.

Finally, a teacher addressing the value of homework—or any class activity as it relates to the so-called "real world"—is problematic. For starters, students are already living in the real world, so forecasting future skills is not accurate or productive. Additionally, the notion of the real world, which will be addressed heavily in Chapter 3, is very subjective and problematic for teachers to use as an incentive or even a threat with students.

The obvious alternative would be to not draw attention to the students who didn't complete their work. Shaming students in front of their classmates, or anyone for that matter, is never acceptable. Something as simple as chatting one-on-one after class or placing a note on a desk is more effective than public shaming.

SKETCHING OUT SOLUTIONS

➡ SOLUTION ONE: CREATE A CLASSROOM THAT WORKS FOR ALL STUDENTS

Creating a classroom that works for all students takes time and is achieved through intentional actions. It is not something that happens simply by making a seating chart and sticking a poster with an inspirational quote on a landscape image. Classrooms that work for all students are a combination of physical elements, procedures, and culture.

> ### CREATING A CLASSROOM THAT WORKS FOR ALL STUDENTS
>
> » Organize furniture and physical space with students in mind
> » Create rules with students' input
> » Reinforce positive behaviors
> » Enforce expectations and follow-through

While not all teachers will have control over the furniture in their classrooms, most are able to determine the arrangement. Are kids sitting on islands by themselves or in clusters or pods? How much space in the room is "teacher space" and how much is student or shared space? Are the walls filled with student work and spaces for them to share their learning?

Consider utilizing a class meeting or class discussion to solicit and gather input from students. Brainstorm freely, then put all ideas on a board or chart paper. Lead a discussion on each proposed rule or expectation. Push students to think about why you need a particular rule.

Too many rules and expectations are simply lists of "don't do this" or involve the word "no" throughout. This puts the focus of student behavior as a negative one that must be curbed. Yet if you write the rules or expectations as positive behaviors to strive for, the message is that you expect good things from your class.

Finally, it is so important for teachers to follow through on expectations and rule enforcement. Too often kids see their peers treated differently, and this breeds resentment and mistrust. While there are always expectations, all students need to be treated fairly.

⇨ SOLUTION TWO: LEVERAGE RELATIONSHIPS TO ENGAGE STUDENTS

Step one in building relationships with students is to treat them like people. If our teacher, Mr. Pape, had regular dialogues with his students, he probably would have known these particular students were history buffs. Knowing your students' interests can be used to design learning activities they will connect with. This goes beyond content interests and into all aspects of who they are as people. For example, if you have a student who is interested in filmmaking, let them create films to demonstrate their understanding. Viral movements such as the Twitter hashtag #IWishMyTeacherKnew, born from the work of Kyle Schwarz, is a great example of how critically important it is to get to know the nuanced worlds our children live in.

Another great way to leverage student relationships is to provide a forum for feedback, and there are many ways in which teachers can do just that. The most obvious form of feedback for many teachers comes through the formal administrative evaluation process. While this can help, it often falls short of making true change in practice. However, teachers who reach out to both students and parents often receive more rich and meaningful feedback than those who don't. Students especially provide brutally honest feedback about their experiences in a classroom. Providing an outlet for students to share their thoughts allows a teacher to demonstrate that they care about their students' opinions and value their thoughts. This can be done through one-on-one conversations, class discussions, or even surveys.

Simply providing an opportunity for students to provide feedback is not enough, however. Follow-up and follow-through are important. If you are going to ask for feedback, you must act on it. That is not to say you do everything a kid asks, but it must at least be acknowledged. If students share frustrations over a common experience, the teacher would be wise to have a class discussion addressing it. While not everything can be changed, having the discussion fosters trust among the students. They must know their feedback has been heard and is something the teacher values.

⇨ SOLUTION THREE: BUILD POSITIVE RELATIONSHIPS WITH STUDENTS

There are so many simple things a teacher can do in order to build and foster positive relationships with students. Above all else, recognize that students are people who have lives outside of their schools. As we saw with three of the students in this chapter, some of our students have tough lives. Recognizing what students are going through and what they carry with them is a crucial first step to building positive relationships. As Mrs.

Rain said in the teacher's lounge, "Get to know the kid before teaching the student." The only way you can get a glimpse into your students' lives, and therefore understand them, is to form positive relationships.

SAY HELLO EVERY SINGLE DAY TO EVERY SINGLE KID.

This is so simple and yet very important. Touch base with every kid every day. One year I had a student who was the stereotypical "quiet girl" who sat in class and spoke only when spoken to. I made it a point to say hello to her every single day she walked into my classroom. At one point in the spring, she shared with me that I was likely the only person who knew her name. I laughed it off and told her that plenty of people surely knew her name. She went on to tell me that she has days where she leaves her house, goes to school, comes home, and the only person to say a word to her was me. While this is incredibly sad, it speaks to the power of just noticing kids and making the simple connection.

ENGAGE WITH STUDENTS OUTSIDE OF THE CLASSROOM.

The key is to engage with students in a setting outside of a classroom. A wise man once told me that if you engage in fun or play-based activities outside of the classroom, the child will connect you with the activity. You will no longer be the teacher who is always asking for work or making them take notes but will be the person who plays dodgeball, chess, music, etc. Find something outside of the classroom setting to engage in with students.

TALK TO THEM.

Talking to students seems like a no-brainer and something all teachers do. However, that is not always the case. Many teachers talk to kids about their work or their behavior in class, yet the key is to engage students in conversations beyond the classroom to show you care about them as people. A simple question about their weekend can go a long way in establishing the grounds for a positive relationship. Yes, teachers need to find a balance between caring and invading privacy, but talking with students is key.

DON'T YELL.

As soon as a teacher raises his or her voice, a student will be put on the defensive and, in many cases, shut down. Teachers should always talk to students in a calm manner without showing anger or frustration. This is especially important for students who have experienced trauma or verbal abuse outside the school setting. Kids will feed off the emotion of the teacher, and they are more likely to bond with teachers who are compassionate and calm.

HAVE EMPATHY.

Too many students, like those in the story, have lives filled with incredible difficulty and stress. I have encountered students who are facing challenges at home that I as an adult would struggle to deal with and overcome. As a teacher, one way to build strong relationships with kids is to listen to them, be there for them, and be understanding of their lives and those things outside of their control.

MAKE LEARNING FUN.

Students will gravitate toward and engage with teachers who make the learning in their classrooms fun. When kids are little, learning is a joyful act driven by curiosity. Teachers who can create learning that is fun will have a higher chance of student buy-in and, as a result, foster positive relationships.

At the end of the day, teachers have many things on their plates. From new initiatives and higher demanding parents to shrinking budgets and political pressures, teachers are overwhelmed. They are often expected to do more with less. Every school year we have students in our classes who refuse to do work, misbehave, act out, or simply don't want to be there. This is a reality, no matter where or what you teach.

There are a lot of things we as teachers will attempt to address those problems, such as class rules and incentives, but gold stars and candy will only get us so far. Others will try to punish and reprimand students into submission. Again, this will not always work and often creates more problems than we started with. The single greatest tool a teacher has at their disposal is the creation and fostering of positive relationships. Relationships alone have a greater impact on teacher success, which then translates into student success.

THINKING BEYOND THE FRAMES

» What steps are you taking in your classroom to intentionally build positive relationships with your students?
» What type of student do you find you struggle the most to connect with? What does this indicate about you as a teacher and how can you grow from it?

TO THE DRAWING BOARD

» Sign up to sponsor or supervise an intramural sport, club, or other activity to create and foster positive relationships with students outside your classroom.
» Create a schedule for regular class meetings with student input and discussion.

SEND TO THE FRONT OFFICE

If you are an administrator, there are a few things you can do in order to facilitate positive relationship-building in your school. First, be a model of positive relationships yourself. Treat all staff fairly and get to know who they are as people beyond who they are as teachers and extended staff. The way you treat assistants, cafeteria workers, custodians, and bus drivers indicates that you value all stakeholders in a child's learning.

Another big action is to be visible in your hallways and classrooms. Teachers and students should see you as a member of the school family. Interact with students and staff, both in an official capacity and a social one. Make sure staff and students see you in the building and not just in your office. One of my favorite administrators to keep tabs on is Tim Lauer, a veteran principal in Washington state, who regularly roams his school taking pictures and talking to kids about their learning. I love following his Instagram (@timlauer) posts highlighting the great things in his school and his obvious pride in sharing it.

RESOURCES

Hare, Rebecca Louise, and Dr. Robert Dillon. *The Space: A Guide for Educators.* EdTechTeam Press, 2016.

Schwartz, Kyle. *I Wish My Teacher Knew: How One Question Can Change Everything for Our Kids.* Np: Da Capo Lifelong Books, 2016.

IT WILL HAPPEN...

Yes, kids will fart in your class. Consider yourself lucky if that's the worst thing that happens in a day. Other bodily functions can—and will—happen right in your classroom. Depending on your resolve, some of them might come from you. I had a long-standing "puke-free" streak in my classroom before it was finally broken after twelve years. It happens. The thing to remember is, this is a horrible thing for a kid. It is moments like these that often brand a kid for life. I still recall a kid I went to school with whose nickname from second grade on was related to a particular stain he left on a classroom carpet. Do whatever you have to do to draw attention away from a kid who has had an accident. If things get bad, you can pull a Billy Madison and join in the kid's embarrassment.

IT WILL HAPPEN...

Yes, you will have a student, a class, or multiple classes you just don't like. This is the truth. I can name a handful of students right now who have pushed my buttons, and I did not look forward to seeing them on a daily basis. Some were mean, and others were lazy. There were even a few that just bugged me, though I never entirely figured out what it was about them that did. The key here is that these kids can never know they get to you. Teachers must treat every kid fairly, and students should never feel as though you are singling them out because of your feelings towards them. Trust me, this is not always easy, and some kids make it harder than others. Anyone who says you need to like all your students clearly hasn't been a teacher. You won't like them all, but you must respect each one and treat them all fairly.

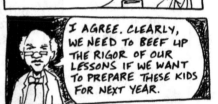

27

I BALANCE STUDENT CHOICE WITH MAKING SURE THEY ARE EXPOSED TO THE CONTENT. **BALANCE** IS THE KEY.

IT IS OKAY FOR STUDENTS TO HAVE FUN AND **EXPERIENCE JOY** WITH ONE ANOTHER.

29

SEEK REGULAR **FEEDBACK** FROM STUDENTS AND PARENTS.

THE BEST DATA IS **CONVERSATIONAL** AND **OBSERVATIONAL**

R egardless of your students' age or what content area you teach, you will be given some sort of curriculum or list of topics you must cover, and your students will be assessed on that material. This may come in the form of state assessments, district assessments, or even the classroom assessments given at the end of terms. By and large, the data from these assessments is used to evaluate not only the students but also you as the teacher. Most school systems have some level of student data as part of a teacher's evaluation. The data from these assessments drives much of what happens in schools today from district initiatives and teacher evaluations to student placement and professional development plans.

FRAMING THE PROBLEM

● PROBLEM ONE: DATA-DRIVEN DECISIONS

I know haters will jump out of the woodwork at this, but I dislike the phrase "data-driven decisions." When it's used in a meeting, bile rises in the back of my throat. I know data is important. It allows us to place students in courses most appropriate for where they are academically. In addition, it can give us insights into the type of learner a student is and therefore plan our support and resources accordingly.

That being said, let's look at the data we are using to drive our decisions. In most schools, the data held above all else are math and reading scores. For most, those are the only subjects tested on the state tests and often the scores used in teacher evaluations. Science, social science, and even elective courses are being manipulated to support student learning and increase scores in math and reading. For years, as a social science teacher, I felt we were the forgotten child within the curriculum family.

On one hand, data is important and can be used to help students in a myriad of ways; however, in far too many schools, an overreliance on data has created systems where students are reduced to numbers and percentages highlighted on spreadsheets. If we know our work is about the kids, then maybe we need to shift our focus a bit. Even Mrs. Smith and her counterparts in the comic are frustrated with their students' scores and have what could be seen as a bit of an unhealthy obsession with them.

SKETCHING OUT SOLUTIONS

⇨ SOLUTION ONE: BALANCE

If you were to look at the curriculum you are tasked with covering in a given school year, what percentage would you feel kids would need know down the road, whether five, ten, or even twenty years from now? If I'm being honest, when I look at much of the content I teach, I think very little will be of significant value beyond late-night trivia at the local bar. That is not to belittle the content we teach or devalue our curriculum, but the reality is that a vast majority of the curricular maps are not worth the paper they are printed on once a kid leaves that class and moves on.

Moreover, how much of our content can a child simply Google? While a child's future area of study might determine the value of those courses, I'm sure most functioning adults can look back at our school years and reminisce about the many wasted hours learning content we didn't need once the tests were over. With that in mind, we have to balance what kids may or may not need later with what we know they will all need. Thankfully, Mrs. Smith has Mrs. Coffman, who shares some of her insights into providing balance—such as providing choice within the required content.

Yes, kids need exposure to curriculum and access to learning new content. More importantly, there are skills all kids need regardless of what path their lives take. I was once sitting at a table with CEOs of Fortune 500 companies as part of the annual meeting of the Business Council. The folks I was sharing a meal with made more per minute than I do in a year as a teacher. We discussed skill sets they look for in future employees. Whether it was Michael Dell or Riley Bechtel, both tycoons in their industries, they all looked for similar skills in their employees—and creative problem-solving, collaboration, and resilience were high on all of their lists. None of them were concerned with test scores or GPAs. They want folks who can work together, solve problems, and keep moving forward despite failures and setbacks. Those are skill sets we need to balance within our content in schools because all students, regardless of their path or vocation, will need them for life.

⇨ SOLUTION TWO: JOYFUL LEARNING

A friend of mine, Dean Shareski, who is an educator with thirty years of experience working with both teachers and students, often talks about the value of having joyful experiences with students. He argues that even if particular activities in schools are not aligned to standards or preparing for some grander outcome, if they are filled with joy, they still have value. Sometimes we create activities for students that we know are fun but other times, they sneak up on us and moments of joy are created on their own. They are hard to explain, difficult to plan, and nearly impossible to measure.

One day a teacher came to me and told me she had a lesson plan fall through and wondered if the kids could come to the library and read for the period. Of course, I said yes and the thirty-plus eighth graders settled into the library. I could tell they were burned out on reading, given the week of standardized testing they had just completed. So I pulled out our Keva planks and had them complete some building challenges just for fun. The kids had a blast and really got into the challenges. As we neared the end of the period, I gave them the final challenge of seeing how tall of a tower they could build. It was then that the "moment" started taking shape without my knowledge.

A group of boys started building and were making some great progress with their tower. It swiftly reached five feet, then seven feet, and then topped ten feet. As the period wound down, the boys kept building, and we let them. The bell rang and the boys kept going. Kids began spilling out of classrooms and stopped to watch the tower being built. As the tower reached the eleven-foot mark, the boys reached out to taller classmates to come over and join in the build. It was awesome. Almost the entire grade level was circling the tower and cheering on the boys. It was a moment of joy to remember. The boys decided to end their build and knock their tower down to thunderous applause from their peers and teachers.

To take it a step further, the group asked if they could come in at lunch to build a tower that touched the ceiling, which is around fourteen feet tall. Naturally, I said yes, and they showed up to build again. They chose this activity over being in the lunch room hanging out with their peers because they were having fun. This time we had to bring in a ladder, and they succeeded in touching the ceiling, just as their classmates returned from lunch. Again, their efforts were greeted with applause and high fives.

Building the tower started out as an activity to kill some time and give kids a break from testing and reading. It was just for fun. Yet it became more than that for these kids, and I guarantee they won't forget that moment any time soon. Joyful learning is not something that will show up on an assessment or evaluation and not something you can measure. In fact, it is even hard for me to put into words the moment created by and for these kids. It's was just one of those "you know it when you experience it" moments.

As teachers, we need to be better at recognizing when these moments are taking shape and let them happen. At one point, I will confess, a teacher stepped out and yelled at the kids to get to class during the passing period. I am also happy to confess the kids didn't listen and went on cheering on their classmates with the full support of every other teacher in the library. Joy has value, and we should encourage more of it.

⇨ SOLUTION THREE: SOCIAL AND EMOTIONAL LEARNING

Taking care of a student's social and emotional learning is just as, if not more, important than the content in our curricula. We see Mrs. Coffman on page six of the comic interacting with a student who didn't finish their work. Clearly this student had something going on in their personal life standing in the way of finishing the work. Rather than reprimand or even discipline the student, Mrs. Coffman simply asks questions and listens to the student. Mrs. Coffman understands that if this student's social and emotional well-being is not taken care of, the content and curriculum of the class will be pointless and irrelevant.

How a child develops the skills within an SEL framework impacts their long-term success both in school and in life. It is essential for students to not only be exposed to SEL activities but also explicitly taught SEL skills. According to the Collaborative for Academic, Social, and Emotional Learning (CASEL),

> "Social and emotional learning (SEL) is the process through which children and adults acquire and effectively apply the knowledge, attitudes, and skills necessary to understand and manage emotions, set and achieve positive goals, feel and show empathy for others, establish and maintain positive relationships, and make responsible decisions" (casel.org).

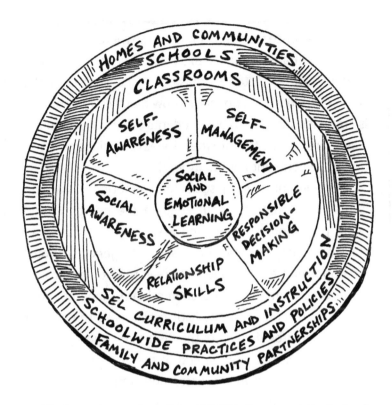

The image is an adaptation of CASEL's Framework for Systemic Social and Emotional Learning, created independently from CASEL. To view the original image, please visit: casel.org/core-competencies.

The five skills embedded with the SEL wheel can be integrated into any and all curricular areas. The CASEL network offers a vast repository of resources and strategies to embed these skills and teach them intentionally. Research indicates schools that implement an SEL curriculum have outcomes of improved interpersonal relationships among students, more positive feelings toward self, and a reduction in problematic or risk-taking behaviors.

I'm a science teacher in Minnesota, where high-school biology is infamous for the extreme number of standards students are expected to master in one year. Over the years, I've found that no matter how much course content is crammed into a syllabus, students learn more (and are way more fun to teach) when I weave social and emotional elements into our daily work.

For me, integrating social and emotional learning is first and foremost about keeping the heart in mind while preparing, teaching, and assessing lessons. I plan class activities that encourage student agency, scaffolding opportunities for students to lead their own learning. For example, my biology students learn many of those standards through case-study discussions. At the start of the year, I'm providing all of the discussion questions and reference materials. By the end of the year, students are looking up their own resources and framing their own questions. Whenever my instructional choices empower students to choose what they learn, their self-regulation skills and sense of personal responsibility grow.

While teaching, I'm careful to use inclusive, friendly, and authentic language. My goal is to communicate to my students that I'm glad they're there. I learn their names, use their names, and try to give each student a sincerely welcoming greeting every day. In a million microconversations, I learn about my students' passions and foibles. In doing so, I'm building positive relationships and modeling interpersonal skills. Simultaneously, I build in varied but structured group work tasks so that students can practice these skills right away. For example, when learning about cells, students are assigned specific group roles (micro-scope technician, logistics manager, safety officer, etc.) to view pond microbes with their peers. The next day, students might be building models of cells, using a different approach so that students with different strengths can shine. Everyone always has a job that's necessary and valued, and through their completion of these jobs, students recognize and reveal their gifts.

—**Megan Olivia Hall**, 2013 Minnesota State Teacher of the Year

 ## SOLUTION FOUR: CLASSROOM CULTURE

I often ask groups of teachers I work with, "If students had the option to leave your class when it wasn't meeting their needs, would they?" This is a tough question because many of us are fearful of what the answer would be. To be fair, I wouldn't suggest doing this in kindergarten, as we would likely have a great many little people wandering the halls. However, this question tells us a great deal about our classrooms. Yes, there are lessons I taught in ancient world history that many kids didn't really get into. It is tough to excite the masses about the struggle between the patricians and plebeians in ancient Rome. If kids had the option that day, many would have likely headed for the exits.

The content we teach is only a small part of the equation. The culture we create in our schools and classrooms is even more important. Are we creating spaces so open, welcome, and engaging that our students want to be there, regardless of the potentially disinteresting content of the day? Do we have classrooms like Mrs. Coffman's on page six where students are lining up and excited to enter? There are often a few characteristics present in classrooms with positive cultures.

POSITIVE CLASSROOM CULTURES

POSITIVE RELATIONSHIPS

The most important element of building a positive classroom culture is having positive relationships with students. It's so important that we've dedicated a chapter of this book to it.

RESPECT

Establishing respect is crucial. Respect goes both ways: The students must respect the teacher, and the teacher must respect the students. Students must feel their ideas and who they are as individuals is respected and valued. To be clear, respecting your students are not the same as being friends with them.

SAFE SPACE

For many of our students, the school and the classroom are the places they feel the safest. Some come from home environments that are unsafe or just not ideal conditions for children. By and large, we cannot control that, but we can control their emotional and physical safety when they are in our schools.

> ### STUDENT OWNERSHIP
>
> Students will want to be in a classroom where they have
> some skin in the game. They will connect with activities
> where their feedback is taken into consideration, espe-
> cially if they have any sort of control over the process
> or the outcome. If they feel like the classroom is their
> learning space rather than just the teacher's room, they
> will connect and engage.

⇨ SOLUTION FIVE: FEEDBACK

Feedback comes up a lot because it is so important. The more
feedback we can gather as a teacher, the better. It is a source of
professional growth (as outlined in Chapter 6); however, it can
also guide instructional decisions and the day-to-day actions
in our classrooms. This can be done, as demonstrated by Mrs.
Coffman, through surveys and feedback questions on assign-
ments or activities.

I find some of the greatest teachers know how they are being
perceived by their classes. This is a form of feedback that is gathered constantly throughout a teacher's day. There is no way to
track this feedback, but great teachers use it effectively. When
teaching a lesson, are you able to recognize when the students
have "checked out" and then redirect the lesson to pull them
back in? This skill is crucial because without recognizing this
nonverbal feedback, teachers will continue down a path of dis-
engagement and disinterest.

⇨ Solution Six: Look and Listen

As Mrs. Coffman shares on the seventh page of the comic story, the best data is observational and conversational. Now, this is not to dismiss test scores completely or claim they have no value—they do—but maybe they are not the sacred idols we often imagine them to be when we elevate their importance. For example, how many of you can get pretty close to predicting which students will do well on a test before you even grade them? Of course, some kids will surprise us, but the reality is, if we are paying attention, the tests are almost pointless. I feel confident I can sit with a student and have a three-minute conversation and know pretty well what they know and what they haven't quite figured out. Now, I'm sure you are asking yourself, "How do I find time to have three-minute conversations with thirty students?" Simply put, if you pay attention, you can quickly identify those who need the full three minutes, those who may only need thirty seconds, and sometimes those who don't need a conversation at all on that particular day.

"WHEN PEOPLE ARE TALKING, LISTEN. DON'T JUST WAIT FOR THEM TO BE DONE SO YOU CAN TALK."

TO THE DRAWING BOARD

When we look at data, we can learn a lot about a kid. For example, poor reading scores can indicate potential mental or even physical concerns we as teachers need to address. There is real value in knowing these things. However, those scores cannot get at what makes a kid "tick." So much can be learned by simply watching kids while they work and interact with each other. Pay attention to the subtle clues about which kids are not following along or those who are bored because they need to be pushed. In addition, there is nothing more valuable to a teacher than a conversation with a kid. OK, a great contract with a solid salary and health benefits is valuable as well. Yet, to do our job effectively, we have to know our kids, and the best way to do that is to engage them in conversations about their learning and struggles.

THINKING BEYOND THE FRAMES

- » What other data points beyond academic scores can we gather to provide better information about students' growth?
- » Examples include student surveys, nurse visits, physical education data, attendance, etc.
- » How much of your curriculum do you think students will need five, ten, or even fifteen years after they leave your classroom? In what ways does the answer influence your planning and teaching?

» Plan an activity where the main goal is students having fun together. Try playing board games, going on a walk to a park, or letting the students pick something they would like to do as a class.

» Visit the CASEL resource (listed in resource section of this chapter) and create a lesson to teach a specific SEL skill.

Administrators, I hate to break it to you, but in many cases, you are big part of the problem of teachers straying from teaching what matters. For starters, many teachers know student test data is a part of their evaluations. I've seen schools where teachers' scores are posted publicly. We know this practice is not good for students, so it shouldn't be done with teachers. Have honest conversations with the teachers in your school about their data and minimize the importance of singular testing events, such as state tests.

The beauty of administrators is that as much as I give them a hard time about being the cause of a problem, they are often the solution. Great administrators can help refocus teachers on teaching what matters and empowering them to be great for kids.

I'm going to speak out of the other side of my mouth on this one, so bear with me. While data is held in much too high regard in many schools, poor data can at times indicate a problem with the teaching and instruction in a classroom. If students of a particular teacher earn low scores year in and year out, there is a problem, and it needs to be addressed. It is an administrator's responsibility to identify the root of that problem and create a plan of action to improve and fix it.

RESOURCES

"What Is SEL?" Casel, Collaborative for Academic, Social, and Emotional Learning, casel.org/what-is-sel/.

Shareski, Dean. *Embracing a Culture of Joy*. Bloomington, IN: Solution Tree Press, 2017.

IT WILL HAPPEN...

Ask any teacher about that "one parent," and they'll likely recall a story, without blinking, about a parent interaction that went south. I could go on and on about certain parents I've interacted with over the years who, I believe, truly hated me. Some will be angry with you for holding their child accountable. Others will be angry with their child but take it out on you. Even tougher are those split families that want to put you in the middle and take out their family drama on you. I have a few tips that have suited me well with difficult parents. First, always let them vent without interruption. Second, acknowledge their concerns and ask how you can help make the situation better for their child. Finally, and above all, never tell them how to raise their child. If this doesn't help, bring in the big guns and call the administration for backup. They get the big bucks because they know best how to help in situations like these.

IT WILL HAPPEN...

While I hope a teacher never has to deal with the death of a student, it will likely happen. I have seen many students and former students lost to accidents, suicide, and illness throughout my career. It is never easy, and nothing can truly prepare you for it. Teachers handle these things in different ways based on many different factors. When tragedies like this happen, it's important to seek out support for yourself and then attend to your students. Many schools have crisis teams or counseling centers to help students and staff through tough times like these. If not, reach out to local medical of therapy centers in your community.

Motivating kids to do something—especially something they would rather not do—might be one of the more daunting issues a teacher will face. In my career as a teacher, but also in my time as a parent, I've seen a great many things aimed at motivating students. Some worked, while others failed miserably. Personally, I take motivation pretty seriously as I taught ancient world history for thirteen years to sixth graders. I know it will come as a shock to most, but learning about "old dead people" is not high on most twelve-year-olds' lists of things they are enthusiastic about learning. In this chapter, our teacher, Mr. C. struggles with many of the same things I have struggled with personally, as have many of my colleagues.

FRAMING THE PROBLEM

● PROBLEM ONE: INCENTIVES AND PENALTIES

We've all seen incentive and penalty scenarios in classrooms before. Students who complete a task receive stickers. Students who finish their timed math test first receive a piece of candy. Teachers take ten percent off a grade for every day an assignment is late. Classes might earn brownie points for positive behaviors, and when a certain number is accumulated, the teacher brings in brownies. I could go on and on with examples of incentives and penalties teachers have tried in order to motivate students. Personally, I got really good at math in elementary school because when I finished my work, I was allowed play *Oregon Trail* on the computer. For those familiar with the game, yes, I was always frustrated by restrictions on my buffalo-hunting haul.

When we look at incentives and penalties, there are some things we need to keep in mind.

» No incentive or penalty will work for all students. Just like adults, students are motivated by different "carrots." These carrots can range from stickers and bonus points to candy and extra recess time.

» Some incentives/penalties create a divide between the haves and the have-nots. Students who have a particular home life are often more or less likely to fit school and class norms. For example, students who come to school hungry are going to be more motivated by food than students who do not share that same need.

» Many incentives and penalties are public in nature and can create social and emotional problems for students.

⬤ PROBLEM TWO: PREACHING AND CONNECTING TO THE REAL WORLD

Are we preparing our students for the real world?

This question, and its resulting conversation, come up in schools often. How are you preparing your students for the "real world"? When they are in elementary school, we try to prepare them for junior high. When they are in junior high, we prepare them for high school. Finally, in high school, we prepare them for college. Along the way, we strive to prepare our students for the real world, but are we preparing them for something that actually matters or even exists? Better yet, are we preparing students for a world based on what we think they need or want?

Many students live in contexts we as teachers have never encountered—and likely will not ever encounter. Yes, we do our best to empathize and see things from our students' perspectives. However, it is naive to think we can possibly prepare students for, or even help them cope with, the actuality of their real world. We do the best we can, but some students see, feel, and experience things we never will. Some kids are worried about their real world when they're six years old, while others likely don't until long after high school.

In this chapter, our teacher, Mr. C., pontificates about how important learning is for his students. He hopes to motivate the students by telling them he is preparing them for the real world and makes a rather poor attempt to connect it to getting good jobs and so on. I admit, I have been guilty of this in my class more than once.

Telling students we are preparing them for the real world is disingenuous and a bit arrogant on our part. In reality, we are spending our time preparing our students for the next level of their academic careers. Yes, there are some procedural and content-based elements we need to create foundations for within our students. However, we cannot assume it is motivating them by reminding them of this "real world" they will be entering. Instead, we may want to help them navigate the real world they already live in. Maybe we need to do a little less preparing in schools and more learning and living in the precious moments we have together.

● PROBLEM THREE: COMPETITION

A few scenarios in this chapter show Mr. C. resorting to competition, and it does not work out quite like he had hoped. I still remember when my oldest son came home from school and exclaimed that he had won the "math race" that day in class. You know this race. It is the one where kids are given a sheet of twenty math problems, and they must finish it in sixty seconds. The winner is determined by who finishes first. In speaking with him about his joyous victory, I asked him who lost. He gave me another student's name but followed it up with, "But he always loses, so he doesn't even try."

This caused some head-scratching because I always found competition to be a motivator. As an athlete through high school and college, I thrived when I was competing with someone else who could push me. I was always in a position to win or at least be competitive, so would I have had the same motivation to compete if I was in a spot where I didn't have a prayer of winning? Likely no. It makes me wonder how many kids experience situations where competition is a confirmation of their shortcomings.

As I'm sure you can tell, all the problems above are actually solutions within themselves. If used properly, any of the previously mentioned motivational strategies can work. However, they will not work every time for every kid. I've spent a lot of time researching just how to motivate my students. Remember the "old dead guys"? That section was definitely a struggle. One of the best things I did was come across the book *Drive* by Daniel Pink, which delves into the research behind what motivates human beings. Since our students generally fall into the "human being" category, many of his principles apply in our schools. Specifically, he suggests autonomy and choice as being some of the great motivators of human behavior.

Taking those thoughts and expanding on some of my own experiences, I've highlighted six key solutions to the motivation conundrum: choice, collaboration, innovation and passion, relevance, self-competition, and authentic audiences. In this chapter, our teacher comes to these conclusions after his conversation with the drone-building student and his insightful furry friend.

⇨ SOLUTION ONE: CHOICE

This is kind of a no-brainer for many teachers, but it is always worth repeating. Students are motivated when they have some level of choice and agency over their learning. Lots of research supports this, but simple common sense tells us students are going to buy in more when they have some choice, which Mr. C. learns towards the end of the comic.

SIMPLE WAYS TO INCORPORATE CHOICE IN YOUR CLASSROOM

» Let students choose novels they read.
» Allow students to choose the format of their work, such as a poem, movie, skit, or essay.
» Enable students to choose others to collaborate with.
» When doing research, give students a variety of topic options.
» Create ways for students to choose their audience.

⇨ Solution Two: Collaboration

I don't know about you, but working with another teacher on a project is a lot of fun, and I find it motivates me. Of course, it also depends on the teacher. I created this book in collaboration with a friend who is not in the education field. We spend countless hours bouncing ideas back and forth and building on each other's ideas. If you have ever worked on a great team, or in a really effective partnership, you know the power and motivating influence of that collaboration. Students are often demotivated, and even discouraged, when being forced to work alone or with a group not of their choosing.

For our students, collaboration is just as powerful. Most students find collaboration to be motivating. Schools are learning communities, and kids should access the community as part of their learning. If we constantly force students to work alone, why should they bother coming to school? While the makeup of groups and partnerships is crucial, students are generally motivated to create and learn with their peers overall. Even if the partnerships are based on potential friendships rather than academic reasons, as we see with our students on page two of the comic, students are motivated when working with those they choose.

One thing to keep in mind is that some students are not great group members. We assume it's a behavior issue, but in reality, some students just don't know how to be a solid member of a group. Help students through this process by starting with a low-risk activity, such as a group icebreaker. Work with students to create norms, establish roles, and collaboratively complete a task. It's important to teach students how to work in a group in a relatively non-academic setting before raising the stakes into graded or assessed activities.

⇨ SOLUTION THREE: INNOVATION AND PASSION

Our teacher, Mr. C., posits the idea of "Genius Hour" to his students, where kids can delve into learning about things that interest them. For teachers not familiar with Genius Hour, it is a set time dedicated on a daily or weekly basis to students' interests, where they are allowed to spend time learning and creating something based on an interest or passion they have. I love these types of activities and even help with our school's Innovation Day, which is essentially a full day in which students create their own learning projects for the entire day. From the moment they walk into our building, through the moment they leave at the end of the day, they work on their Innovation Day projects. Their only requirements are to learn, create, and share. It's that simple. Students are highly motivated by these types of activities because they are granted autonomy in their learning. Furthermore, when students pursue a topic that interests them, they often learn and engage in content from a variety of their school curricula.

PROBLEM WITH PASSION

One thing to keep in mind is that while allowing students to be innovative and follow their passions is motivating, it is not always a good idea. The reality is, we do have content kids need to learn in order to progress and move forward in their course work. If you have students like me, I would not be choosing to learn more about math (unless *Oregon Trail* was in the mix). However, my teachers knew that I needed to learn the content they put forth for my own educational good. As with anything, balance is the key.

⇨ SOLUTION FOUR: RELEVANCE

I had a conversation with a neighbor one night during which he shared how much he hated math when he was in school. As an adult, he runs a landscaping business, and he uses math every single day. Patio dimensions, angles of plants, and a whole host of other design principles require him to use math on a daily basis. He told me he loves math and would likely have enjoyed it more in school if it was more relevant or connected to something "real." Math teachers spend a lot of time trying to connect math to real life, and yet students may not see the relevancy of determining when two trains will meet after leaving two different stations. Instead, let's give students problems that relate to their lives and therefore have relevance.

It doesn't matter what subject we teach; there are ways to connect the content to students' lives and the world around them. Yes, there are some elements of our curriculum that are easier than others. ancient world history was often a stretch, but I did the best I could to show my students how the Holy Wars of the Crusades built a system of cultural divides that we still see today. We would look at current events happening in the Middle East, where violence or unrest was happening. Then we took those groups of people and geographic elements and traced them back to their origins in the Holy Wars of the Crusades. It helped students not only understand the history of these events, but also provided context for what is happening in our world today.

⇨ SOLUTION FIVE: SELF-COMPETITION

When I was in college, I was on the track team and coached by the legendary Al Carius. By legendary, I mean he has coached for forty-four years and been responsible for thirty-seven team national champions between track and cross country. For all of those years of coaching, he had, and still has, one philosophy: "Run for fun and personal bests." He believed if we enjoyed what we were doing and focused on improving ourselves, that was all we needed to do. I still believe in the power of competition as a motivating factor. However, not all students can compete at the same level. I'm not advocating we give everyone a ribbon and tell each person they are special. We all know that leads to entitlement and a false sense of accomplishment. We can create competitive scenarios where all kids have the ability to win but also celebrate individual growth and success. For example, teachers can create a variety of competitions for which the skill sets needed to succeed will vary. Not every competition should be about finishing first or winning by having the highest score. Maybe a "winner" is determined by the most thoughtful response or the greatest act of humility. Track individual growth by having students chart their own progress and set goals and milestones for themselves. As a teacher, you can celebrate their growth and success as it comes. Mr. C. figures this out on the final page of our comic, when he engages with a young man looking to improve his writing skills.

⇨ SOLUTION SIX: AUTHENTIC AUDIENCES

We may not like it, but our students are more motivated by likes, comments, retweets, and views than by any letter grade we will put on their work. Students are incredibly motivated by authentic audiences. The reality is, their teachers and classmates are not authentic; rather, they're captive audiences. Posting students' work on the web or via social media opens up to a global and, in turn, more authentic audience. In doing this, our students have access to a global perspective on their work and content. Connecting with this global audience may also lead to conversations previously not possible. Students can be motivated when they receive feedback from students in other parts of the world, or even experts in the field.

I think we are, at times, fearful of putting students' work online because of too much *20/20* or *Dateline*. We think if we post a student's video project online, a windowless van will roll up to the school and start snatching kids. However, the reality is we live in a globally connected world where feedback is constant. As teachers we can tap into those connections to provide rich learning experiences. Yes, there is always the potential for negative content or feedback. This provides a great opportunity for learning around how to engage with people online and how to filter content.

When considering sharing your students' work with a global audience, there is always a need for caution and common sense. First, it is important for teachers to know and understand their school's protocols and rules around posting student work. Some schools require parent permission slips to be signed prior to the sharing of any student work. Other schools have a flat no-share policy due to the high number of immigrants within their student population. It is imperative teachers know, understand, and work with their school's policies to provide safe and purposeful sharing of student work.

- » In what ways are you already using choice and collaboration in your classroom learning experiences? Are there ways you can increase these two in order to further motivate students?
- » How are you taking your content and making it relevant for students?
- » Are you placing student work in front of an authentic audience? If not, what are steps you can take in order to achieve this?

Just as teachers must motivate their students, administrators must motivate their staff members. The good news for administrators is that, unlike some students, a vast majority of their staff are motivated individuals, which is why they've chosen to teach. That being said, there are elements within teaching that are demotivating and that can lead to teacher burnout. Number one on that list is a disinterested or unsupportive administrator. The ways in which you support, encourage, and empower your teachers is critical to not just their motivation but also their overall success.

Many of the same strategies of motivation applicable to students can work with teachers as well. Are teachers given choice and autonomy in their professional development? Instead of having teachers "sit and get" during a professional development day, engage them in leading it or provide choices for them based on their needs. When a new initiative is rolled out, are teachers allowed input? Bring teachers to the table via an advisory or leadership group to discuss any and all new initiatives impacting them or their students. How often do administrators seek teacher feedback on what is or is not working in the building? It takes virtually no time to send out a survey to staff or simply chat with your teachers about what is working and what may need to be improved.

All of these strategies can keep your teachers in the loop and motivated. While teachers don't have to agree with ever decision made in a school, their buy-in and support will be much higher when they are included and their voices valued.

To THE DRAWING BOARD

» Plan and implement an Innovation Day at your school or in your classroom.
» Create a choice board with options for students for their next class project.
» Provide a space for students to post and share their work beyond the walls of the classroom.

RESOURCES

Pink, Daniel H. *Drive: The Surprising Truth about What Motivates Us.* New York: Canongate Books LTD, 2018.

Pink, Daniel. "The Puzzle of Motivation | Dan Pink." YouTube video, 18:36. Posted Aug. 25, 2009. youtube.com/watch?v=rrkrvAUbU9Y.

Stumpenhorst, Josh. "Innovation Day." *Josh Stumpenhorst,* 2017, joshstumpenhorst.com/innovation-day/.

IT WILL HAPPEN...

I still remember when a mom approached me one summer and thanked me for saving her son's life. If I'm being honest, I didn't even immediately recognize the woman, and I had no clue who her son was. She proceeded to tell me a story about when her son was in my class in sixth grade. Apparently, during a parent-teacher conference, I shared with her that her son was hanging with some troublesome kids at lunch. I then told her they were not a great influence on her son. Now, to be fair, I've told countless parents this same story, so I was still not sure where the "saved his life" piece was coming in. She went on to tell me she and her husband had some hard conversations with their son (who I finally was able to recall) about his friends. He moved away from that friend group and started hanging out with different kids. At this point I was still confused, but she continued and said the "bad kids" I'd told her about went downhill big time in high school. A couple got really into drugs and at least one was expelled due to fighting and other disciplinary issues. So, she said, "You did save my son's life." The reason this story is important is that is truly illustrates the power of a simple word, conversation, or gesture. Teachers have conversations like these with kids and parents almost daily, and many of them stay with these kids and parents for far longer than we realize. It is important we remember our influence even if we never truly know our impact.

IT WILL HAPPEN...

Sadly, teachers often encounter evidence of neglect or abuse of our students. As a parent myself, I can't imagine a person who can willingly harm their child, but it happens. Depending on your state or district policies, you may be a mandated reporter. Personally, I've made a handful of calls to Child Protective Services for apparent abuse. It's never easy, but a teacher's first job is to take care of the safety of the students in the classroom. Some kids might experience abuse without any physical signs, which is why it is so important that teachers create classroom environments where kids are safe and feel cared for.

in·no·va·tion

MY BIG TAKEAWAY WAS BUILDING POSITIVE RELATIONSHIPS WITH THE STUDENTS AND SEEING WORK WE DO FROM THEIR PERSPECTIVE. EMPATHY IS ABOUT PUTTING OURSELVES IN THEIR SHOES AND CREATING LEARNING OPPORTUNITIES THAT WORK FOR THEM.

ALL RIGHT, Y'ALL!

I FOCUSED ON THE **REFLECTIVE** CHARACTERISTIC OF AN INNOVATOR'S MINDSET.

MS. AMY

"MY FIRST STEP WAS TO KEEP A DAILY JOURNAL. EACH DAY I WROTE DOWN TWO THINGS I DID WELL AND ONE THING I COULD DO BETTER."

"I OBSERVED SOME OTHER TEACHERS' CLASSES."

WOW—I NEVER WOULD HAVE THOUGHT TO DO IT THAT WAY!

ALL RIGHT, MY LITTLE PEOPLE!

BE SURE TO FILL OUT THAT SECTION AT THE BOTTOM OF THE TEST. REFLECT ON THE LEARNING YOU DID BEYOND WHAT WAS IN THOSE QUESTIONS.

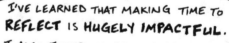

I'VE LEARNED THAT MAKING TIME TO **REFLECT** IS HUGELY **IMPACTFUL**.

I ALSO FOUND VALUE IN EXTENDING THE EXERCISE TO MY STUDENTS. THEIR **INSIGHTS** HELPED THEM WHILE ALSO PROVIDING GREAT **FEEDBACK** TO ME.

97

Far too many people equate "innovation" with something radically new or shiny. The word is too often tossed around haphazardly when a speaker wants something to seem groundbreaking or game-changing. Many people assume innovation only applies to technology or new initiatives. In reality, it is none and potentially all of those things. Innovation truly occurs when we do something either new or better. In education, innovation can manifest in many different ways. Reading *The Innovator's Mindset* by George Couros helped me a lot. I believe the solution to innovation in education lies within Couros's eight characteristics of an innovative mindset.

⬤ PROBLEM ONE: INNOVATION

Yes, innovation—or rather a lack of innovation—is the problem in this chapter. Our teacher in this comic, a curmudgeonly older gentleman, is a prime example of this. Initially, he is only interested in reading the book because it is an evaluation year. (We've all been there.) However, his reluctance to read is based on a number of factors. Initially, he doesn't want to read a book written by someone who doesn't teach in a classroom. This is a reality for many teachers and a valid concern. He eventually comes around, thanks to his impending evaluation and positive peer pressure from his group members, all of whom seem to be enjoying the book. Unlike the anecdotes in the previous chapters, this one goes right for the solution: bringing innovation into our schools and classrooms. Innovation must be treated as more than a buzzword, or it will be a problem. The teachers in our comic learn the value of Couros's book, and, in doing so, discover a path toward an innovative mindset.

SKETCHING OUT SOLUTIONS

George Couros establishes eight characteristics of an innovative mindset in *The Innovator's Mindset*. In the comic portion of this chapter, the teachers engage in what many consider a torturous endeavor: an education book study. However, they quickly learn the value of not only this particular book but also in collegial conversations. It is through these conversations that the teachers deepen their understanding and push their thinking toward innovation. I once had the pleasure of listening to Charlotte Danielson, the creator of the Danielson Framework for teacher evaluation, where she described how conversations are the key to deeper learning. I couldn't agree more. When we engage in conversations around teaching and learning, we gain perspective, challenge beliefs, and evolve our pedagogy.

⇨ SOLUTION ONE: EMPATHETIC

Mrs. P. was assigned the "empathetic" characteristic and started with the question, "Would I want to be a student in my own classroom?" Teachers need to build relationships with their students and have empathy for their individual situations. I firmly believe a teacher must get to know the kid before he or she can teach the student. Without understanding who a student is as a person, we can never hope to connect with them in the necessary way to increase their learning potential. Students will learn and achieve more when they feel valued and cared for by their teacher. Just like Mrs. P. did in our comic, a teacher who simply takes the time to ask students what is or is not working will begin to foster a relationship built upon understanding and empathy.

The power of empathy is often downplayed because people associate it with sympathy, which it is not. In *A Whole New Mind*, Daniel Pink suggests the notion of empathy as "the ultimate virtual reality—climbing into another's mind to experience the world from that person's perspective" (Pink 159). There are certainly times when the thought of trying to figure out what is going on in a child's mind is scary. We can do simple things to understand their perspectives. For starters, follow a student's schedule for a full day. Yes, walk the halls, sit in the uncomfortable desks, and try to use the restroom during a passing period. Experience their day and reflect on that experience. Do a home visit and see what life is like on the outside for that child. There is certainly a logistics issue with physically visiting every student, especially in a junior- or senior-high school setting when you may have one hundred or more students. However, visit those you can and provide other opportunities to bring families into your classroom or school. Give every student the opportunity to show you, their peers, and themselves

LEADERSHIP IS ABOUT EMPATHY.

IT IS ABOUT HAVING THE ABILITY TO RELATE AND TO CONNECT WITH PEOPLE FOR THE PURPOSE OF INSPIRING AND EMPOWERING THEIR LIVES.

OPRAH WINFREY

what they are interested in or where their passions lie. Anything you can do to put yourself in a kid's shoes, no matter the size, is going to be a good outcome.

⇨ SOLUTION TWO: PROBLEM FINDER

We want to be able to help our students become problem finders. A problem finder is someone who simply looks for their own problems to solve rather than always having the problems dictated to them. Problem finding is tough in our current education landscape of standardization and data obsession. Due to jam-packed curricula and overtesting, many of the problems students are asked to solve are ones given to them by their teachers. We need to work toward providing time and guidance for students so they can identify and solve their own problems. Too often these types of activities happen in clubs or extracurricular activities.

Mr. Robin takes these ideas to heart as he tries to help students find their own problems, realizing that problem-based learning just isn't good enough. Teachers need to help students create their own problems, rather than just following directions and project plans set forth by their teachers. In my school, I oversee a science club with a colleague of mine. During our club time, students come up with problems or questions that they associate with a local science challenge competition. What they choose to learn, question, and solve is entirely up to them. It is great to see the students dive into the problems and questions they are interested in rather than those that are too often forced upon them in their classes.

So how can teachers help their students become problem finders? For starters, open up your classroom to the community in which they live. Have them identify problems they are interested in finding answers or solutions to. Ask them what they are interested in learning about. Jump into Genius Hour or host an Innovation Day. Being a problem finder doesn't always mean having a problem—a question could just as likely drive them to learning or creating. For example, when studying the fall of ancient Rome, present students with the real-life scenarios and let them figure out not only the problems but work through their own solutions. Toddlers are already good at doing this. They constantly ask questions as they attempt to make sense of the world around them and solve their own little life problems. School eventually sucks that curious, problem-finding sense out of them, and we need to work to give it back.

⇨ SOLUTION THREE: RISK-TAKING

As our curmudgeonly Mr. J. realized, being a risk-taker doesn't mean jumping into every new initiative but being mindful of what works for kids. That being said, being a risk-taker means stepping outside of the norm and trying something new that could benefit your students. A great friend and over twenty-five-year veteran teacher, Rob Hunt, stepped away from traditional

COMING INTO THIS, I THOUGHT "INNOVATION" WAS ALL ABOUT TECHNOLOGY AND SHINY NEW STUFF.

BUT IT REALLY IS ABOUT HAVING A MINDSET FOCUSED ON THE BEST POSSIBLE OUTCOMES FOR THE KIDS!

grades many years ago. He and I worked together on creating a grading system that worked better for us and our students. The system was a risk because not everyone was on board initially. Furthermore, it was different than what parents and kids were used to. In the long run, it helped create a better and clearer system of providing feedback about student learning to parents and kids. Our system offered specific feedback for students and parents around learning standards. Rather than a grade for an essay, students were given feedback on individual elements of their writing.

I still remember when our whole school did a book study around so-called "best practices" in education. While parts of that book applied to some of my students, the vast majority was not applicable to many of them. I could make up a statistic about how different approaches work for different students, but it would not be accurate. However, in my experience, for any one best practice or great lesson, there will always be students who don't connect or fail to follow along. This is why it is so important to take risks and try new and dynamic ways of teaching for the benefit of each kid. Mr. J. discovered the true meaning of this through being open to students trying something new. It can be that simple.

➡ SOLUTION FOUR: NETWORKING

As George points out in the book, "Isolation is often the enemy of innovation" (Couros 53). With that in mind, it is important to create a network where you can go for answers, support, ideas, and guidance. This can happen in your school through systems such as professional learning communities or departments, but it can also happen outside of your building through the use of social media. Ms. Trenton was able to help her colleagues network by creating Tech Tuesdays as a way to come together and share ideas. She even took it a step further in connecting through online spaces. Teachers should find what works for them and helps meet their professional needs, perhaps by leveraging social media for professional development, as outlined in \ Chapter six, "Professional Growth." Teachers can also help create spaces for students to build their own learning networks.

I still recall when the refrigerator was the keeper of my high-quality at home. Yes, parents still hang children's artwork up at home, but kids are creating and doing far more than ever before. Social media has created an outlet for us to share our students' work and content in ways never before possible. Through doing this, students connect and create networks of fellow learners around the globe.

Students today also leverage social media to encourage and create social change. Whether taking to Twitter to protest police brutality or posting images of marches after school shootings, students use social media to build networks of like-minded people who want to change their communities. Some students take to social media to create a space of celebration and to lift each other up. Leyden High School in suburban Chicago, Illinois, and its #LeydenPride hashtag have been a great source of not only sharing news but also celebrating all students. The hashtag is not only utilized by staff but by students sharing, celebrating, and lifting each other up. We can argue about the content students post or the issues they take up, but social media has helped mobilize students, and they have created these networks to bring about social change. As a teacher, we want our students to change the world. When students can network, they are able to effect changes we never thought possible. A quick search of "teens using social media for good" on Google will provide numerous examples of students leveraging social media in a positive manner.

➡️Solution Five: Observant

This should come as a no-brainer to most teachers, but being observant is a big part of being effective, as well as innovative. Yes, we can grow by watching one another teach and observing what our colleagues do both in and outside of school buildings. However, being observant goes beyond the school walls. Mr. Guido comes to the realization and value of observing content and people outside the world of education.

As previously mentioned, Daniel Pink's book *Drive* was a source of inspiration for how I motivate my students. Pink will freely admit his book was written for the business world, yet his work applies to schools as well. Another example would be the work of Sal Khan, who founded the Khan Academy, a free online learning resource to support math instruction. What started as a simple way to help his cousin turned into a dynamic portal through which students can receive content remediation or enrichment. While people argue about the value of Khan's work, millions of students have benefitted from his videos and courses.

Sometimes we shut out ideas or people simply because they are not in a school or a classroom. However, when we do this, we lose out on potentially gaining insights that might impact the work we do with kids. As Mr. Guido in the comic did, who looks eerily similar to the handsome author, we need to seek inspiration from anywhere. Listening to Elon Musk talk about his work can inspire all of us to try new things. There are so many TED Talks to inspire and challenge our thinking. I still remember watching Deb Roy's TED Talk, "The Birth of a Word," in which he discusses how children acquire knowledge. This talk intrigued me and ultimately impacted how I teach literacy. Truly, inspiration can be found anywhere if we are observant.

⟹ Solution Six: Creators

The concept of students as creators is getting more traction in schools than ever before. Ideas spawning out of the maker movement help provide spaces where students can be creators. Many teachers, like Mr. Neil, are allowing students to create evidence of their learning beyond traditional means. Initiatives like Hour of Code, a national program to encourage students to learn basic computer coding, are allowing students to be creative and design their own learning experiences. I still recall visiting New Brunswick High School in New Jersey in 2013 and its maker space, run by Laura Fleming. For me it was odd to see all of the "stuff" spread out in a library space and kids tinkering, fixing, breaking, and building all sorts of things. Laura had created a space were kids could truly create their own learning experiences outside of the curriculum.

For those not familiar with a maker space, it really can be anything that meets the needs of your particular student population. It is a space where students can be creative, innovative, and "make" things. They can be high tech with students building robots, 3D printing, or even using power tools. On the other side of the coin, they can be low tech with students creating with good old-fashioned cardboard and duct tape. There are really no rules or "right/wrong" ways to have a maker space. The key is they are places where students are creators.

Beyond maker spaces and special events like maker faires, which are festivals dedicated to making, kids can and should be creators in their classrooms. Mr. Neil in our chapter displayed this by allowing kids to create evidence of their learning in a variety of formats. As much as we want kids to become problem finders, we also want them to create or find their own solutions. Yes, we need kids to understand content and have foundational skills, but we need to build on those so students can create based on their learning. A great example was the eighth-grade math teachers in my building trying to teach the Pythagorean theorem to their students. I worked with the teaches and came up with an idea of having students use their knowledge of the theorem to create cardboard ramps. The ramps had to follow the rules of the theorem for a right angle. Then the students created prototypes, and we drove out high speed Sphero Ollie robots off their ramps and collected the data. Not only was it fun, but they were creating within their learning experience.

⇨ SOLUTION SEVEN: RESILIENCE

If you are being innovative or just trying something new, you may be met with resistance. Change is hard and, often in schools, people work hard to protect certain legacies (e.g., projects, activities, or programs that have existed for a long time). As our cookie-baking teacher Mrs. K. finds out, it's important to stick to it and push for change if it will help our students. In my first years of teaching, I did whatever I was told by my fellow teachers, especially those in leadership positions such as team leaders or department heads. I wanted to go with the flow and not cause any issues. However, as I became more confident—and tenured—I started changing some things. I started by making small changes, such as deciding not to assign a novel that had been done for years because I thought it was outdated and didn't suit my students' needs. I changed projects that had been done since the dawn of the ditto machine. Slowly but surely, I pushed back on some of the things "we'd always done." Eventually, I worked with my colleague Rob Hunt, and we essentially changed the entire way our English classes were taught, giving the students greater ownership of their learning. Likewise, in our story, Mrs. K. comes to the realization that she has to try new things on behalf of her students and recognizes it won't always be easy.

The other aspect of resilience worth mentioning is fostering resilience within our students. If I'm being honest, many kids can't handle failure or things not going their way. On page eleven of the comic, Mrs. K. has a student who says they have tried "seven times" but can't seem to get it. Rather than give in and provide the student with an easy out, she steps back and encourages the student to keep trying. Too many parents and teachers want to protect students from failure because we are afraid of

"IN ORDER FOR
MY CHILDREN TO
BECOME MASTERPIECES,
THEIR FLAWS MUST BE
ALLOWED TO REMAIN, AND
SERVE AS AN ESSENTIAL
PART OF THEIR TALE."

—JESSICA LAHEY,
THE GIFT OF FAILURE

harming a student's self-esteem or emotional well-being. While that is admirable, it actually robs the student of opportunity to develop resilience. The long-term effect of this is hugely problematic. Students who are not allowed to fail at an early age don't develop the coping skills needed to navigate the bigger and more consequential failures inevitable later in life.

➩ SOLUTION EIGHT: REFLECTIVE

Ms. Amy is our reflective teacher from the comic, and she does it well. Being a reflective teacher simply means being aware of what is working and what is not. A reflective teacher intentionally makes time to reflect on all aspects of their teaching. Practices such as keeping a journal or peer observation (discussed in Chapter six) are particularly helpful tools in a reflective teacher's toolkit. To take it a step further, I want to share a great five-question activity from Jennifer Gonzalez, "The Gut-Level Teacher Reflection," which she shared on her blog *Cult of Pedagogy.*

1. Look around your classroom (or picture it in your mind). What parts of the room make you feel tense, anxious, or exhausted? What parts make you feel calm, happy, or proud?

    After considering all parts of your room, pick two to three hot spots that need the most attention. These should be your priorities for change.

2. Open up your plan book (or spreadsheet or wherever you keep your lesson plans from the year) and just start browsing, paying attention to how you're feeling as your eyes meet certain events. What days and weeks give you a lift when you see them, a feeling of pride or

satisfaction? Which ones make you feel disappointed, irritated, or embarrassed?

Try to find common themes or patterns. What changes do you need to make so you feel less stressed about your workload, and more satisfied about how you design your students' learning experiences?

3. Take a look at your student roster. What do you feel when you see each name? Which names make you feel relaxed, satisfied, and proud? Which ones make your chest tighten with regret? Which ones make your stomach tense?

Once you have identified some themes in the relationships you have with your students, choose two to three areas where you need to grow. Consider collecting student feedback in a systematic way next year.

4. Mentally travel from classroom to classroom, picturing each teacher in the building. What are your feelings as you approach each one? Which coworkers give you a generally positive feeling? Which ones are neutral? Which ones make you feel nervous, angry, or annoyed?

After going through the faculty and staff, choose a few people with whom you need to change your relationship, whether by repairing it, limiting it, or nurturing it.

5. Look at the following professional practice "buzzwords." As you read each one, do you have positive, negative, or mixed feelings? What other words have you heard a lot this year that give you a strong feeling one way or the other?

- » technology
- » differentiation
- » data
- » research-based strategies
- » Common Core
- » higher-level thinking
- » flipped learning
- » standards-based
- » student choice
- » PLC

If any of these words give you negative or hard-to-name emotions, chances are you're feeling insecure about these topics. The struggle may be caused by policies you have nothing to do with, or they may indicate an area where you need to grow. If it's the latter, this is an opportunity to take one weakness and face it head-on— make it a priority to develop your skills in that area.

Jennifer's five questions are a great way to reflect on our practice as educators. She goes on to specifically state that once you go through these questions, you should develop an action plan. While reflecting is important, it should always lead to action. Like Jennifer, Ms. Amy can take all of the feedback in the world from her students, as well as observe her fellow teachers. Yet, if she does not take action to improve her own teaching, it will be a waste of her time.

THINKING BEYOND THE FRAMES

» What systems do you have in place to solicit feedback from students in order to better understand their perspective?
» Which of the eight characteristics present the greatest opportunity for growth for you? Which one do you feel is a strength for you?

TO THE DRAWING BOARD

» For this chapter, I wanted to make a list of things to try based on the eight characteristics of an Innovative Mindset.
  » **Empathetic** – Participate in a home visit with one of your students.
  » **Problem Solver** – Allow your students to participate in Genius Hour or Innovation Day (or something similar).
  » **Risk-taker** – Toss out an old unit plan and try a new approach or new project idea.
  » **Network** – Join a social media site and build a professional learning network.
  » **Observant** – Watch Dan Pink's Ted Talk about motivation and read his book *Drive*.

» **Creator** – Instead of assigning a paper-and-pencil test, let students create something to demonstrate their learning.
» **Resilient** – Identify one small activity or project that has "always been done" and make the decision to stop doing it. Create a list of reasons to support your decision in case of colleague pushback.
» **Reflective** – Go through Jennifer Gonzalez's "The Gut-Level Teacher Reflection."

SEND TO THE FRONT OFFICE

For starters, all administrators could do well to grab a copy of George Couros's book, *The Innovator's Mindset,* and give it a read. It goes well beyond the eight characteristics and provides sound advice and practical strategies for building a culture of innovation within a school. Specifically, it is important to support innovative teachers who are trying something new. It takes guts to take a risk, and often these teachers are ostracized by their colleagues. For some reason, many teachers find it threatening when a fellow teacher tries something new or stands out in a different way. I'm not sure if this comes from a place of jealousy or a feeling of incompetence. When I see a teacher doing something awesome and outside the box, I want to check it out and learn. However, some teachers think differently and feel that the teacher is showing off or creating an unfair standard to which they will be held. Administrators should support those outside-the-box thinkers and protect them from the naysayers.

Whenever I have a teacher who is wanting to try something different, I say yes in any way, shape, form, or fashion that I can I say yes. I let them know that I hope it's an evolving process and that they can step back and reflect on what's working and what's not working . . . but that I'm always willing for them to take chances. I also try to share tweets, articles, and books that I hope encourage them to take risks, as well as teachers that are doing different things that are more innovative than what I may see typically in a classroom. By sharing those out-of-the-box examples, I hope they see that I am willing to have those kinds of spaces and places in our building. They also know that at any given moment if I see these risks negatively impact our academic instruction, we have to have a conversation . . . It's not a no-holds-barred environment; academic integrity is at the core of what we do.

—**Amber Teamann**, Whitt Elementary principal
in Wylie ISD in Wylie, Texas

RESOURCES

Couros, George. *The Innovators Mindset: Empower Learning, Unleash Talent, and Lead a Culture of Creativity.* San Diego: Dave Burgess Consulting, 2015.

Danielson, Charlotte. *The Handbook for Enhancing Professional Practice: Using the Framework for Teaching in Your School.* Alexandria, VA: Hawker Brownlow Education, 2009.

Gonzalez, Jennifer. "Gut-Level Teacher Reflection." *Cult of Pedagogy.* June 7, 2014. cultofpedagogy. com/ gut-level-reflection-questions/.

Pink, Daniel H. *A Whole New Mind: Why Right-Brainers Will Rule the Future.* New York: Riverhead Books, 2012.

Roy, Deb. "The Birth of a Word." March 2011. TED video, 19:45. ted.com/talks/deb_roy_the_birth_of_a_word#t-523820.

IT WILL HAPPEN...

I have seen some random stuff come out of our school cafeteria over the years. A student once brought us a piece of pizza with what appeared to be a drywall screw embedded in the crust. We've seen hot dogs with unnatural color schemes and rice that defies the laws of matter. What is the lesson here? Really, there isn't one. It is just a reminder that when you think you've seen it all, you most certainly have not.

IT WILL HAPPEN...

Every so often, a kid will come into your class to complain or gripe about another teacher. There are two things you can take away from this. First, it's positive that they trust you enough to vent about another teacher, so consider that a compliment on the relationship you have built. Second, the relationship you have built may, in fact, be too close, as they've likely lost sight of the teacher-student boundary. While you should reflect on the complaint, you should not entertain it, even if you agree with the student wholeheartedly. Whenever this has happened to me, I thank the student for sharing and suggest they have that conversation with their parents.

Writing about technology can be difficult because so much the technology is obsolete before the ink is dry and, before we know it, we are moving on to the next gadget, gizmo, or gimmick. Personally, I love technology. It allows both students and teachers to do things previously impossible (or at the very least difficult). However, when it comes to technology, we need to be mindful of the *why* before the *how*. If we don't know why we want or need a new technology, there is a problem. Far too many technology initiatives start with the *how* before the *why*, which often leads to poor implementation and wasted resources. Our teacher in the comic, Ms. Lighthouse, surely started out with the *how* when writing her grant and stumbles as she tries to discover her *why*.

FRAMING THE PROBLEM

● PROBLEM ONE: MORE TECHNOLOGY = MORE LEARNING

When technology enters a classroom, many of us—teachers, parents, and students—assume the learning will automatically increase or improve somehow. In reality, that is not the case. If my lesson is bad, adding technology is not going to make it better. In fact, in many cases it will be worse. The best analogy I can think of is one that all middle-school teachers will know well. When that stinky boy comes back from gym class and douses himself in body spray, it doesn't actually make him smell better. In fact, it's quite the opposite. In that same way, a stinky lesson is a stinky lesson. Ms. Lighthouse learns this right away and commiserates with her fellow teachers on page six of the comic.

Many schools have jumped to one-to-one initiatives (i.e., providing a device for every student). There are ranges of devices in use, such as iPads or Chromebooks, and frankly most people will argue their preference. However, far too many of these initiatives fall into the same "more technology = more learning" trap. Basically, teachers are just digitizing old worksheets into PDFs, and kids are making digital dioramas disguised as interactive posters. Simply putting a device in every child's hand is not going to magically increase test scores or shift learning into new spaces.

● PROBLEM TWO: EXPENSIVE TOYS

This is a real struggle many teachers face, and, in some cases, it is a good one to have. When a new product comes out, we get excited like a child with a new toy on their birthday. We *have to have it,* and once we get it, we give it to the students to play around with. Kids are good at playing. We see this in our story with Ms. Lighthouse, when she gets the robots and 3D printer. Kids are just goofing around and playing. She didn't really have a plan for how to use it in the class setting. This is both a problem and a solution.

When my school first got Sphero robots in our library, the students loved taking out ramps and just playing. It was fun, but no learning was taking place, and we essentially had expensive rolling balls. The same thing happened when we got a 3D printer. We spent time just trolling around Thingiverse.com looking for cool stuff to print. There was really no connection to the learning in their content area courses.

Having said all that, there is a good element to the "playing with toys" problem. Sometimes when kids are playing, other aspects of learning are happening. For one, they are gaining an understanding of that technology, which inevitably increases their technology literacy. In addition, there is a social and emotional piece being tapped into when kids are playing. In our standardized, test-crazed school culture, it's good to just relax and have some fun once in a while.

● PROBLEM THREE: MYTH OF THE DIGITAL NATIVE

"Young people are better at technology." Have you heard that statement? It is a statement that perpetuates the myth of the so-called "digital native." The concept of the digital native suggests the idea that because kids or even teachers are young, they must be good at technology. This just isn't true and frankly is a myth. Yes, there are students who teach me about coding or building drones, but I also have students who need my help to install an app or even understand how to use the home button on an iPad. When we assume all kids are good with technology, we miss opportunities to teach valuable skills and lessons.

There is also inherent bias with the digital native myth. Many students simply don't have access to technology at home. This can be due to a whole host of reasons, from religious to socioeconomic to culture to lack of access. When we assume all kids are good with technology, we make an unacceptable assumption, as our students come from a variety of cultural, social, and financial backgrounds.

● Problem Four: Digital Saturation

Many schools have started to provide devices for all students. My own school district has made that move, and all students walk into school with a device. Initially, the kids, parents, and teachers were pretty excited about this decision. The pilot classes tested out a variety of devices, and when the decision was made, it was met with positive optimism in general. However, a couple of years in, a resistance of sorts has begun. Teachers are starting to push back a little against what I call "digital saturation."

In the comic, Ms. Lighthouse's students are getting frustrated and want to take a break from their screens. A quick search of "harmful effects of screen time" will produce ample research suggesting kids spend too much time on screens. Students today are hyper-connected, largely due to the proliferation of smart-phones. The expectation of students to read, write, annotate, and create nearly all of their school work digitally only exacerbates the problem.

SKETCHING OUT SOLUTIONS

⇨ Solution one: Have Fun

I previously identified kids goofing around and having fun with new technology as a problem, but the reality is, a certain amount of play is not only a good thing—it is essential. For starters, allowing kids to play around with new technology helps them get excited about using it, as well as start learning how to use it. If you get a new robot, pull it out of the box and let the kids play around with it. It helps them develop their technology literacy and gets them thinking about ways to use it. Nearly every single piece of technology I've acquired in my classroom or library has been put into students' hands before I had even figured it out myself.

One great example was a new CNC desktop router machine that we added to our school's maker space. When it showed up, I'd barely figured out how to turn it on, let alone design something to cut into a piece of wood. I gathered a handful of my eighth-grade students, and we problem-solved it and learned how to use it together. It was a great learning experience for all of us. Another time, we created an arcade console. As a fan of the classics such as *Donkey Kong* and *Pac-Man*, I thought it would be a neat project to build a system for our school. Not having a clue how to do this, I grabbed another group of kids, and we did the research together. Our end result was a Raspberry Pi console that played all the great, classic games from the seventies and eighties. Additionally, we designed and 3D printed a gaming controller, complete with joysticks and buttons we wired ourselves. At the end of the day, these two things that started out as just pure fun led to deep technology learning.

In addition to gaining technology literacy by having fun, technology can bolster social and emotional learning. This type of learning, known in Edu-speak as SEL, is getting more and more attention in schools. Personally, I feel this is a good move—students' social and emotional well-being should be valued. When kids are playing or having fun with technology, they are building those skills. Wendy Ostroff, a development and cognitive psychologist, considers play a "motivation propeller." She considers play a natural setup for learning because kids use play and fun as a way to explore their curiosity. Having fun together is critically important to developing positive social interactions and over-all health.

A great example of the SEL component with technology was our Battle Bots tournament. Many of you may be familiar with the show on television where engineers create robots to "battle to the death." I decided to do something similar in my school—minus the flamethrowers and hydraulics. Instead, students were given a plastic cup and a round Sphero robot. The robot would go inside the cup, to which they would add their own body armor and weapons. The most common weaponry we saw were tooth-picks, cardboard bumpers, and popsicle sticks. After their robots were complete, the kids drove the robots into each other and tried to knock over their opponent and render them incapaci-tated. It was a ton of fun! The entire time I was able to work with students, discussing how to work together as well as how to win and how to lose in socially appropriate ways.

SOLUTION TWO: FIND BALANCE

As previously mentioned, our school district moved to a one-to-one device initiative with seemingly high rates of success. However, many students—and even more teachers—have grown frustrated with the pressure of using a device daily, let alone every class period. Sometimes when schools institute new tech-nology, they shame teachers into using it. This creates a situation where teachers feel compelled to make everything a technolo-gy-centric project or activity.

I once worked with one such teacher who felt pressured to use technology. One day, this teacher was excited about a new project involving the cart of iPads. She was all excited about using the iPads and having students complete a "technology project," but when I finally asked what the kids were working on, the answer was, "Flashcards." Now, don't get me wrong, I've got nothing against flashcards. The problem was the kids could take them home to study, print them off, or put them in the cloud (because Google Drive didn't exist yet). However, when I asked the teacher why do this activity that took longer than usual, and frankly was not as useful to the students, the answer was, "But I used the iPads!" I think there are many teachers out there like this who feel pressured into using technology for all the wrong reasons. When this happens, we lose our balance.

I like how Ms. Lighthouse in our comic decided to take the kids outside, even though the kids argued over whose idea it was. Pulling the plug and going outside are great ways to recharge and take a step back. There are also many other things a teacher can do in order to restore that balance, such as periodically assigning work or activities that require no technology. Instead of creating a discussion board online, gather the kids in a good old-fashioned crisscross-applesauce circle and talk to each other. I love that even though our students have access to online books, they still want to come to the library and read a book they can hold in their hands.

⇨ SOLUTION THREE: BE INTENTIONAL

Instead of simply using technology just to use it, we have to be intentional with our use. Personally, I am a fan of the SAMR model, which helps distinguish among types of technology use in the classroom. The model was first shared by Dr. Ruben R. Puentedura as a way to help educators utilize technology.

SAMR stands for:

» Substitute–Technology acts as a direct substitute, with no functional change

» Augment–Technology acts as a direct substitute, with functional improvement
» Modify–Technology allows for significant task redesign
» Redefine–Technology allows for the creation of new tasks, previously inconceivable (Puentedura 2014)

It clearly identifies different use of technology and provides a guide to instructional technology use.

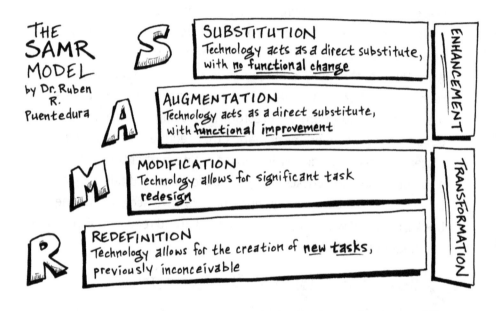

THE SAMR MODEL
by Dr. Ruben R. Puentedura

S SUBSTITUTION
Technology acts as a direct substitute, with no functional change

A AUGMENTATION
Technology acts as a direct substitute, with functional improvement

ENHANCEMENT

M MODIFICATION
Technology allows for significant task redesign

R REDEFINITION
Technology allows for the creation of new tasks, previously inconceivable

TRANSFORMATION

I appreciate the SAMR model because we can identify how technology is being used, which leads to more intentional use. It is important to remember that this is not a hierarchy but rather a spectrum of technology use. Some folks assume we should all aspire to redefinition, but that is not accurate. There should be a healthy balance among all four types of use.

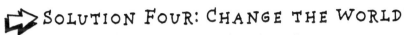# Solution Four: Change the World

Technology can do some pretty amazing stuff, including changing the world. Yes, I know that sounds dramatic but hear me out. As a history teacher, I felt my greatest responsibility was teaching my students how to understand the world around them. This world extended beyond the suburban bubble many of them have lived in their whole lives. I'll go a step further and claim the biggest problem plaguing modern society is a lack of understanding and empathy. I think technology can go a long way in addressing both of these.

Students in maker spaces across the US and abroad are using 3D printing technology to design and build prosthetic limbs for children. Organizations such as Enabling the Future work with schools and other organizations to provide a way for creators to get their designs into and onto the hands and arms of kids in need.

> They are people who have put aside their political, religious, cultural, and personal differences—to come together and collaborate on ways to help improve the open source 3D printable designs for hands and arms for those who were born missing fingers or who have lost them due to war, disease, or natural disaster.
>
> —enablingtheuture.org

Another great example of this is Pernille Ripp's Global Read Aloud program (theglobalreadaloud.com). She had a vision of kids around the world reading a common book and discussing it with one another. It was such a simple idea, but it had profound implications. Through social media, video conferencing, or good old-fashioned phone calls, kids in suburban Chicago or rural Kansas can connect with kids in urban Los Angeles or Sao Paulo, Brazil. When a kid can connect and learn with someone who looks, speaks, or believes differently than them, they gain a perspective that ultimately leads to empathy and understanding. So, yes, I believe technology can empower our students to change the world.

Participating in the Global Read Aloud connected my students and I to participants in many other places. My students are from an at-risk, urban area. Many never leave home, which means they are never exposed to other cultures, demographics, and/or geographical areas. Through our involvement in the Global Read Aloud, we met others from across the country. By connecting using a common piece of literature, my students learned about the United States on a deeper level that was not possible previously. Coming from our area, students had numerous false assumptions about the world around them. Using the Global Read Aloud as a platform, we (educator participants and student participants) changed their perspectives. We now had friends from many diverse areas we could discuss literature and other topics with. Students feel safe to discuss since we all have a common piece of literature to focus on. The Global Read Aloud was a stepping stone to deeper conversations. My students learned about their country on a profound level that was not possible before our involvement in the Global Read Aloud. I have only participated with my classes for two years, but definitely plan to continue. I know my future students will gain insight about the world around them. I hope to help students synthesize their perspectives using the Global Read Aloud classroom connections. I witnessed perspectives transforming previously and know there are more to come.

—Jillian Sosnowski, fourth grade teacher, Lafayette Elementary School, Hammond, Indiana

THINKING BEYOND THE FRAMES

» How do you find a balance in your classroom or school to avoid digital saturation?
» What have your students done with technology that has excited or inspired you?

SEND TO THE FRONT OFFICE

Technology is an ever-changing beast, difficult to both manage and keep up with. Teachers try to master what works for their age groups and subject areas, yet it is nearly impossible to assume an administrator will be up-to-date on technology at their schools. However, they have to know enough to know when it is being used effectively. The only way you do this is by spending as much time as you can in classrooms where the technology is being used. See it in action and talk to the teachers and kids about how it helps their learning. I suggest all administrators grab a copy of *Digital Leadership* by Eric Sheninger for a clear pathway for being a technology literate leader.

RESOURCES

"Enabling The Future." *Enabling The Future,* e-Nable Community, enablingthefuture.org.

Ostroff, Wendy L. *Understanding How Young Children Learn: Bringing the Science of Child Development to the Classroom.* Alexandria, VA: ASCD, 2012.

Puentedura, Ruben. "SAMR Model." Ruben R. Puentedura's Weblog, 2014. hippasus.com/rrpweblog/archives/2014/11/13/SAMR_FirstSteps.pdf.

Ripp, Pernille. "The Global Read Aloud." *The Global Read Aloud,* 2018. theglobalreadaloud.com/.

Sheninger, Eric, and Yong Zhao. *Digital Leadership: Changing Technology for Change-Savvy School Leaders.* Thousand Oaks, CA: Corwin, 2014. A SAGE Company, 2014.

IT WILL HAPPEN...

Depending on how long you work in a particular school, you will likely work with numerous administrators. Between principals and assistant principals, I've lost count of how many I've worked with. As the image suggests, I did work with one who was a Yeti when it came to being out of their office. When kids spotted this individual, they were not sure what they were seeing, and others often dismissed the sighting as the florescent lights playing tricks on them. That being said, I have worked with some outstanding administrators who I was sad to see leave. At the end of the day, if you stay in a building long enough, you will likely "outlive" your administrators who tend to come and go. If/when you have a rough one, just close your door, teach your kids, and hold the fort down until the storm blows over.

IT WILL HAPPEN...

I once took a dodgeball to the face. At the time, I was wearing glasses. The ball split the frames and cut my nose. I can still see the mammoth eighth-grade boy who hurled the ball in my direction. To this day, I recall that as a watershed moment in my relationship with students. I'm not saying you need to take a heater to the face, but you should take a step outside the classroom because playing, connecting, and interacting with students in a different environment is powerful. It allows kids to see teachers as more than just the person harping on their work.

PROFESSIONAL GROWTH.

Where it all began...

First year teaching...

TWENTY-SEVEN YEARS LATER...

If you are like me, you often think about your first year of teaching. I still recall the names and faces of many of those students because there is something special about your first class. However, if you are also like me, you would go back and apologize to each and every one of those students if given the chance. There were so many things I did as a teacher back then because I didn't know any better. I suspect many of you are the same. I know I've grown in general, and I continue to grow as a teacher. As I work with educators, both young and old, I often face the question, "How do we get better as teachers?" My hope is to take a look at the actions of our teacher in this chapter and break down some of her successes and failures.

FRAMING THE PROBLEM

● PROBLEM ONE: TEACHING THE WAY YOU WERE TAUGHT

Identifying Mrs. W.'s problem is simple. She is a stereotypical teacher in that she always loved school and dreamed of being a teacher from an early age. This is true for many teachers. There are a lot of us for whom school was easy—we were good at playing the school game. We became teachers because school was a positive experience, so it made sense for us to continue down that path. Yes, there are others who become teachers as a result of horrible schooling experiences and aim to protect children from similar fates. I consider myself in the middle, as I had some teachers I try to emulate but also those who provided a healthy list of examples of things I would never do with students.

In this chapter, Mrs. W. is truly going through the motions, yet we get a sense that she does love her job and wants to do well. Even as she rolls her lesson plan book over from year to year, she seems to be doing the best she knows how. Early on in my career, I was in the same boat as her. I took the lesson plans that were given to me from a colleague and ran with them. I didn't question or deviate from them because that was all I knew. Every single action our teacher does in this chapter reflects something I did. I assigned a single novel to the entire class, gave forced-choice tests, did in-class grading, and avoided any feedback from students or parents. At the time, it was all I knew.

If we know the problem is "teaching the way you were taught," based on our prior experiences, how do we change? How do we shift away from doing things the way we've always done them and become better teachers? What can we do in order to grow as professionals?

SKETCHING OUT SOLUTIONS

⇨ SOLUTION ONE: FEEDBACK AND REFLECTION

> WE DO NOT LEARN FROM EXPERIENCE...
>
> WE LEARN FROM REFLECTING ON EXPERIENCE.

I'm not big on quotes, but John Dewey's words stick with me. In life, we have experiences that can shape who we are. However, the learning is more pronounced when we reflect on those experiences. This is true for our students, but even more so for us as teachers.

As teachers, we should make reflection an intentional part of our practice. To start, we have to seek feedback. I can keep a journal or speak with a friend or my spouse, but there is an inherent problem with this form of reflection. It is based completely on my experience, and therefore my bias comes into play. As teachers, we teach a lesson, but without feedback from someone else, we can only reflect so much. I've had plenty of lessons I thought went really well, but the feedback from students was not in line with my impressions. One-sided reflection can be helpful, but it often just reinforces what we already believe or want to believe.

Seek feedback from your students and their parents. For me, the number one source of feedback I want is from my students.

FOUR QUICK WAYS TO GET FEEDBACK FROM STUDENTS

» Put a question on the bottom of a test asking for their thoughts on that particular unit of study.

» Create an anonymous form for students to fill out at the end of each quarter seeking input on projects, instruction, or concerns.

» Hold focus groups with students on a regular basis for informal conversation.

» Have comment cards that kids can fill out and place anonymously in a box/tray.

Second to students, parent feedback helps me reflect on my teaching. Early in my career, I did everything I could to avoid parents. If I was in the store and saw a parent of one of my students, I would think, "I don't need toilet paper that bad," and turn around and head out. Yet parents are an incredibly powerful source of feedback. We make assumptions about what our students are going through and how our class impacts them when they walk out our classroom doors, but the parents live it every single day. They can provide insights on what is really going on. We have students who will never share their concerns with us despite our best efforts, and it is through parent feedback that those students' voices can be heard. Personally, I advocate for sending home parent surveys at least once a quarter. Keep in mind, parents who are likely to provide feedback will be those with concerns or questions. Take their feedback with a grain of salt but understand there are kernels of truth in just about all feedback.

As I seek feedback from students and parents, there are three things I like to keep in mind.

YOU MUST RESPOND

I often think of the beloved book *If You Give a Mouse a Cookie* when discussing feedback. If you ask someone for feedback, you better be prepared to respond to it. If a majority of my students are sharing with me that something is not working for them, I need to respond. To be clear, responding does not always mean changing or getting rid of something. Sometimes the response is simply leading a discussion with students about why we do certain things. This can be a great way for teachers to reflect and reaffirm the work we are doing.

Conversely, if something does not sit right with kids or teachers, responding is one hundred percent necessary. Administrators who seek feedback from staff but do nothing with the input are doomed to have an environment where trust is lost and negativity will breed. The same goes for teachers who ignore the feedback of students. It doesn't take long for kids to realize their voices don't matter and their thoughts are not valued. Change based on feedback is not always imperative, but a response certainly is.

TRUTH HURTS

If as teachers we can't handle the tough truths, we may not be cut out for the work. Mrs. W. gets hit with some hard truths when she gives her students the survey. What would your reaction be if a kid said your class was the worst part of their day? How about the parent who emails you to say your communication is lacking and makes them feel left out? If a colleague criticizes a project you've come up with, how will you react? What will you do when your student test data indicates your students are not making enough growth compared to your colleagues' classes?

These are all forms of feedback teachers often receive. It has been my experience that the best teachers are those who look at each one of them as an opportunity to learn and grow. Rather than make excuses or place blame, they own the feedback and take steps to move forward and improve.

CONSIDER THE SOURCE

When we reach out and gather feedback, we have to be careful when thinking about the source. Yes, I know I just said we have to take the feedback seriously even if it hurts and we don't like it, but we also have to be mindful that some people are never happy—and that includes kids. We will always encounter those who are unhappy with our work, and we can't take every single comment, note, or feedback personally. We must view every element of feedback as an opportunity to learn about ourselves or the person who left the feedback. Both will lead to a deeper understanding of the work we are doing.

As teachers, we often ask our students to reflect on their learning and, in many cases, get feedback from their classmates. If we know the value of this practice, we must embrace it as educators when we truly want to improve what we are doing. There will be times when the feedback will hurt. There will also be times when the feedback will reaffirm the great work we are doing. Both have a value, and teachers must seek out both. The practice of seeking regular feedback, along with reflection, helps us grow both personally and professionally. If we do it right, we will not need to get a DeLorean to travel back in time and apologize to any more classes.

➡ SOLUTION TWO: POWER OF PEERS

Like students and parents, our peers are great sources of professional growth. By "peers," I am referring to those people you work with in your subject area department, in your grade level, and within your classroom—your colleagues. All of these people can be great sources of inspiration and motivation. Yes, I intentionally left administrators off this list. Your school principal will likely conduct formal evaluations and offer you feedback. However, the principal is not with you on a day-to-day basis, but rather a few select observations when the dog and pony show is on display.

As Mrs. W. learns, having a peer mentor, while initially potentially awkward, can yield benefits for all teachers. I think about every professional athlete in the world. What do they all have in common? They have peers who they learn from and with. Regardless of whether it is a teammate on a basketball team or a sparring partner in the boxing ring, they all have peers to help them achieve greatness. Teaching should be no different.

Leveraging your peers as a source of growth can be powerful, but it can also be daunting. Gathering feedback from colleagues is a tougher element to tackle. The bottom line is, we don't typically like honesty in education. Teaching is a deeply personal endeavor; as a result, we take things personally. It is really tough to have a critical conversation with a colleague who is also a friend, so I am a big advocate of peer observation. Find a trusted friend in your school and ask them to come and watch you teach. Give them something specific to look for and then have a follow-up conversation about what they observed. Start small and consider focusing only on the positive things going on your classroom. Once you've established that trust, work toward the tougher conversations about what isn't working or potential areas of growth. You can also set up a camera and record yourself teaching. Yes, this might feel awkward at first, but it can be really beneficial and a safe first step if you fear jumping right into peer observations.

Jason Flom, an educator from Florida, created a helpful list of five ways to establish productive peer-to-peer observations:

1. WHAT IS THE ESSENTIAL QUESTION BEING OBSERVED?

Albert Einstein once wrote, "If I had an hour to solve a problem, and my life depended on the solution, I would spend the first fifty-five minutes determining the proper question to ask . . . for once I know the proper question, I could solve the problem in less than five minutes."

Essential questions play a similar role in schools. With a focused line of inquiry shaping peer-to-peer observations, both the observed and the observer are more likely to take away transformative insight that positively affects instructional practice and student learning.

Additionally, pre- and postdiscussions about an essential question can provide educators with an opportunity to dig deeper—something many of us don't have enough time to do—and help ensure the takeaway from the observation is applicable and relevant.

2. ARE THE ESSENTIAL QUESTIONS FOR THE OBSERVATION CREATED WITH A TOP-DOWN OR BOTTOM-UP APPROACH?

What do our students need from us to learn? Administrators often have general questions that they would like to explore and discuss as a school. For example:

>> As a school, where do we most need to grow in order to further actualize our mission?
>> Do all students feel safe, respected, and welcome on campus? How do we know?

However, a top-down approach to creating essential questions—that is, administrators dictating questions to be discussed and observed—is not the most effective way to begin the peer-to-peer observation process. Administrators should pose questions to stimulate inquiry and solicit teacher insight, ultimately leading teachers to determine their own essential questions based on the priorities they feel are most pertinent to their students. Administrator questions should not serve as vehicles for a hidden agenda but rather as opportunities for teachers to engage in discussion, generate ideas, and create essential questions. These essential questions should then be used as the foundation for peer-to-peer observations.

Teachers are more likely to fully embrace the opportunities afforded by peer-to-peer observations when they have played a role in identifying the essential questions to be investigated and observed—that is, when a bottom-up approach is used. Administrators need to find ways to give teachers an authentic voice when developing the questions that matter to them, their students, and their practice.

Curious about developing essential questions? Check out *Essential Questions* by Jay McTighe and Grant Wiggins. Although the book is geared toward essential questions to help promote deeper understanding for students, it also includes valuable insight for educators working with educators. In the first chapter of *Essential Questions*, the authors help the readers distinguish between essential and nonessential questions. The book even provides a list of questions, which can be easily adapted into a variety of settings and context.

3. WHAT IS THE SCOPE OF THE OBSERVATION?

The questions, "Are our students thriving with our math program? How do we know?" can lead to several different types of peer observations.

As the questions are unpacked by a teacher team, the focus may be on the continuum of the curriculum, from the youngest to oldest students, and their success overall. Or it might be on how the students engage in math on a daily basis. Or both.

The type of observation will depend on the focus. Would it be better for teachers to observe one class during a single lesson, or to organize a walkthrough, which visits a greater number of classes? Both may elicit valuable evidence, but the data captured will be very different.

4. WHAT IS THE PURPOSE OF THE OBSERVATION?

Just getting together to watch each other teach can be unnerving. However, when there is a clear purpose and mutual trust among teachers, everyone can benefit—both the observed and the observers.

However, before entering into any peer-to-peer observation, the focal point of the observation needs to be crystal clear. Are we looking at teacher actions, student behavior, or both? Are observers watching for personal learning or to gather data as part of a study? Are we trying to understand instructional practices or student engagement? Are we watching all students or specific ones?

Answering these questions prior to an observation creates a transparent and safe environment for teachers, who may feel under the microscope and vulnerable when peers come to observe.

5. WHEN IS THE TIME?

For peer-to-peer observations to work, there needs to be time—time to meet and establish the goals of the observation; time to plan the observation; time to find/develop the protocols and tools to use during the observation; time to conduct the observation; time to debrief after the observation; and time to implement changes based on the evidence/knowledge gathered during the observation.

Expecting teachers to just use their already-limited planning time will result in a less fruitful experience and is likely to be met with resistance. With this approach, observations will not be sustainable. Teachers need to feel that observations are a key part of how they improve their practice, not one more thing they have to do.

Thus, it is important that sufficient time, separate from standard planning time, is allotted for observations on a regular basis. The results will speak for themselves, especially over time, as teachers make their practice public with each other" (Flom 2014).

⇨ SOLUTION THREE: SOCIAL MEDIA

Few things have changed my own professional growth like social media. As with Mrs. W.'s mentor teacher in our story, she found inspiration, ideas, and resources through her connections on social media. Yes, the social media tools and apps will change, but the need for, and positive impact of, social media will not.

One of the most amazing things about using social media is connecting with teachers around the world. Beyond that, you can connect with scientists, historians, authors, and even celebrities. All those connections help build your own professional learning network, which is not bound to the walls of your school. These connections have direct impact on student learning experiences.

In addition to connecting with other educators, you can find experts in fields of study connected to your content. For example, I once tweeted out to Reed Timmer, a meteorologist, from Discovery Channel's show *Storm Chasers*.

Josh Stumpenhorst @stumpteacher   7 Sep
I have a Ss who is a huge fan of
meteorology. Wonder if I could get
@reedtimmerTVN to skype him for a
short interview
Expand ↰Reply 🗑Delete ☆Favorite

I had listened to Reed speak at a conference and loved what he had to say. He spoke passionately about his life's dream of learning about weather and everything that goes with it. I had one student in particular who was highly interested in weather and was a fan of Reed. My hope was to get Reed to Skype in for a short interview that I could record and show to the entire grade to kick off our Innovation Day. However, that was not what actually happened.

Instead, the power of social media unleashed itself and, within a short amount of time and a few dozen tweets, I was in a meeting with personnel from Discovery Education. Together, we planned an actual site visit and activities with Reed Timmer. Fast-forward to when Reed drove nine hours through a February snowstorm to visit our school and deliver a keynote speech to kick off Innovation Day. It was a powerful learning experience for our students made possible purely due to social media.

I believe that out in the world somewhere, somebody is doing the exact same job as I am, and they are doing it better than me. My goal is to find those people and learn from them. Every time I hop on Twitter or Instagram, I am amazed at the incredible things teachers are doing in schools. Education is truly an amazing profession and, thankfully, some great folks share it with the world daily. If we want to grow as teachers, we need to see new, different, innovative, and empowering teaching in practice. Social media provides a window into spaces where this work is happening, and I can take a look without ever leaving my couch.

Beyond simply exposing yourself to new ideas, social media can help increase perspective through diverse and varied content. As a teacher in a predominately white school, I lack the perspective of teachers in urban settings; I don't experience what they struggle with on a daily basis. Being connected to teachers in all types of school settings and communities allows me to gain a deeper understanding of all student experiences—both good and bad.

THINKING BEYOND THE FRAMES

» In what ways do you currently seek feedback from students and/or parents? How else can you gather feedback?
» What questions can you ask your students that could lead to growth for you as a teacher?
» How can you help foster a culture in your school where peer-to-peer observation is the norm?
» In what ways do you think you can utilize social media for your own professional growth?

TO THE DRAWING BOARD

» Create a generic survey for students to take at the end of each grading period or term.
» Meet with a colleague or two and create a plan to observe each other and share feedback.
» Join an online network to learn from and share ideas.

SEND TO THE FRONT OFFICE

Teachers are constantly "developing" professionally, and administrators drive the bulk of that development. For the administrators reading this, know that you have tremendous influence over teachers' experiences and outcomes. My question for administrators would be the following: "How are you involving teachers in the planning, implementation, and reflection of their professional development?" Like students, teachers need choice and autonomy in their learning.

There are a number of really simple things an administrator can do in order to ensure successful professional growth among staff. First, seek staff input in a variety of forms, whether face-to-face conversations or a survey of some sort. Second, provide time and space for teachers to learn and collaborate, both formal and informal. Third, recognize that teachers desire to see nontraditional forms of professional growth, such as social media or possibly an EdCamp. Finally, just be open and honest with teachers when it comes to state, district, and federal initiatives you must implement and push down to teachers.

As a building principal, I believed one of the most important aspects of my role was to ensure there was high-quality instruction in the classroom. I worked with some phenomenal educators over the years, so I focused on how I could share what great things were occurring in their classrooms. I used staff meetings to highlight best practices by inviting teachers to share an effective instructional strategy with their colleagues. I found that the information was received much better when it came from a teacher than me as the building principal. That way, it felt like an invitation to try something new instead of a mandate, and it expanded the opportunity for teachers to take ownership of their learning.

Additionally, my entire district administrative team conducted informal walkthroughs, and we provided immediate feedback to teachers in the form of a format we called, "I Notice/I Wonder."

The "I Notice" part of the feedback consisted of things we saw during our brief visit, such as if learning targets were posted, what student engagement looked like, what types of questions were asked by the teacher, and what type of instructional strategy was in place, for example. Instead of asking questions, we used the phrase, 'I wonder.' These statements created opportunities for teachers to reflect on their work, and a majority of them responded to our feedback via email or brief conference within a day or two of the observation.

I used staff, department, and leadership team meetings to ask reflective questions tied directly to our building initiatives, which ensured all professional learning opportunities were relevant to teachers. Finally, I surveyed teachers on a monthly or quarterly basis to ensure we were meeting their professional learning needs.

—**Dwight Carter**, former award-winning principal in central Ohio and current education consultant

RESOURCES

Flom, Jason. "*Peer-to-Peer Observation: Five Questions for Making It Work.*" Paper presented at the ASCD Inservice, October 6, 2014. inservice.ascd.org/ peer-to-peer-observation-five-questions-for-making-it-work/.

BOOK

INNOVATION IS ABOUT HAVING A MINDSET FOCUSED ON THE BEST POSSIBLE OUTCOME FOR KIDS.

TECHNOLOGY IS AN AMPLIFIER OF BOTH THE BEST AND WORST IN TEACHING.

THE ONLY WAY WE GET BETTER AS EDUCATORS IS BY SEEING AND EXPERIENCING BETTER.

CONNECT, LEARN, AND GROW WITH EACH OTHER.

Our goal is for this book is to raise questions which lead to conversation and ultimately action in your classroom and school. Reflecting on each chapter, what are specific things you can take away and implement tomorrow, regardless of your role in your school?

CHAPTER 1 What is one action you can take to build stronger relationships with your students?

_____

_____

_____

_____

_____

_____

CHAPTER 2 How can you ensure decisions are kid driven, rather than data driven?

_____

_____

_____

_____

_____

_____

CHAPTER 3 In what ways will you implement more choice and autonomy in your classroom?

_____

_____

_____

_____

_____

_____

_____

CHAPTER 4 Which aspect of an Innovator's Mindset will you take on and how will you do it?

_____

_____

_____

_____

_____

_____

_____

CHAPTER 5 How will you ensure technology use is intentional and enhances student learning?

_____

_____

_____

_____

_____

_____

_____

_____

CHAPTER 6 List at least one thing you will do in order to expose yourself to new ideas about teaching and learning.

_____

_____

_____

_____

_____

_____

_____

_____

SHARE YOUR THOUGHTS AND IDEAS! #DRAWN2TEACH

Bring Josh Stumpenhorst to your school or event

Josh Stumpenhorst has had the privilege of presenting at numerous local, state, national, and international conferences and workshops. He tailors his presentations to the groups he is working with and provides not only relevant educational research but more of a real-life approach. Josh's goal is to share his own teaching and learning experiences, hopefully sparking discussions that ultimately improve learning and teaching.

Popular Messages from Josh Stumpenhorst

Typically, Josh's presentations are tailored to your event. However, here is a sample of popular keynote sessions Josh has done in the past.

- » Revolutionary Teaching
- » Innovation Day
- » The Future-Ready Library
- » Drawn to Teach
- » Student Motivation

Connect with Josh

Twitter: @stumpteacher
Email: stumpteacher@gmail.com
Web: joshstumpenhorst.com

MORE BOOKS FROM

IM PRESS

EMPOWER

WHAT HAPPENS WHEN STUDENTS OWN THEIR LEARNING

BY A.J. JULIANI AND JOHN SPENCER

In an ever-changing world, educators and parents must take a role in helping students prepare themselves for *anything*. That means unleashing their creative potential! In *Empower*, A.J. Juliani and John Spencer provide teachers, coaches, and administrators with a roadmap that will inspire innovation, authentic learning experiences, and practical ways to empower students to pursue their passions while in school.

LEARNER-CENTERED INNOVATION

SPARK CURIOSITY, IGNITE PASSION, AND UNLEASH GENIUS

BY KATIE MARTIN

Learning opportunities and teaching methods must evolve to match the ever-changing needs of today's learners. In *Learner-Centered Innovation*, Katie Martin offers insights into how to make the necessary shifts and create an environment where learners at every level are empowered to take risks in pursuit of learning and growth rather than perfection.

UNLEASH TALENT
BRINGING OUT THE BEST IN YOURSELF AND THE LEARNERS YOU SERVE
BY KARA KNOLLMEYER

In *Unleash Talent*, educator and principal Kara Knollmeyer explains that by exploring the core elements of talent—passion, skills, and personality traits—you can uncover your gifts and help others do the same. Whether you are a teacher, administrator, or custodian, this insightful guide will empower you to use your unique talents to make a powerful impact on your school community.

RECLAIMING OUR CALLING
HOLD ON TO THE HEART, MIND, AND HOPE OF EDUCATION
BY BRAD GUSTAFSON

Children are more than numbers, and we are called to teach and reach them accordingly. In this genre-busting book, award-winning educator and principal Brad Gustafson uses stories to capture the heart, mind, and hope of education.

Take the L.E.A.P.

Ignite a Culture of Innovation

By Elizabeth Bostwick

Take the L.E.A.P.: Ignite a Culture of Innovation will inspire and support you as you to take steps to grow beyond traditional and self-imposed boundaries. Award-winning educator Elisabeth Bostwick shares stories and practical strategies to help you challenge conventional thinking and create the conditions that empower meaningful learning.

About the Illustrator

Trevor Guthke is a sometimes art teacher and all-the-time artist who honed his skills at the University of Illinois. He has a truly sketchy day job involving spreadsheets. He is a family man with one beautiful wife, three ungrateful kids, and one willfully destructive dog. This book is his first-ever project that has any value to society whatsoever.

ABOUT THE AUTHOR

Josh Stumpenhorst is a junior-high learning commons director in suburban Chicago, IL where he lives with his wife and two sons. He holds a master's degree in curriculum and instruction as well as a National Boards Certification in early adolescence social science. His work as a classroom teacher has earned Josh many awards and honors at both the state, national, and international level. However, his greatest pride is in the recognition given by the students and parents who he works with every day.

Stumpenhorst is an active blogger at joshstumpenhorst.com and Twitter user at @stumpteacher. He is the author of *The New Teacher Revolution: Changing Education for a New Generation of Learners*, which analyzes current practices in schools and suggests alternate and more effective strategies for all teachers.

CPSIA information can be obtained
at www.ICGtesting.com
Printed in the USA
FSHW021905170319
56314FS